LOUD FAST WORDS

T0160322

loud
fast
words

SOUL ASYLUM
COLLECTED LYRICS

DAVE PIRNER

Minnesota Historical Society Press

Special thanks to Jeneen Anderson, Jill McLean, Jim Metz, and Josh Leventhal.

Images on pages 4, 5 (both), 21, 31, 63, 73, and 189 from Minnesota Historical Society collections.

mnhspress.org

The Minnesota Historical Society Press is a member of the Association of University Presses.

Manufactured in the United States of America

10 9 8 7 6 5 4 3 2 1

♾ The paper used in this publication meets the minimum requirements of the American National Standard for Information Sciences—Permanence for Printed Library Materials, ANSI Z39.48-1984.

International Standard Book Number
ISBN: 978-1-68134-172-9 (paper)
ISBN: 978-1-68134-174-3 (e-book)

Library of Congress Control Number: 2020930294

This and other Minnesota Historical Society Press books are available from popular e-book vendors.

This book is dedicated to anyone and everyone
who ever inspired a lyric

CONTENTS

INTRODUCTION

S o, this is the beginning of the spinning of the yarn—a yarn that is me. It's twisted, tangled, fucked up; but somehow you continue to try to knit a sweater, while at the same time not really taking credit for the sweater, and hoping that it will make someone feel warm and better. But somewhere in my subconscious, or my ego, or whatever you want to call it, I wanted to tell my own story. Storytelling is an evolution of something that is passed down and degraded, or upgraded, depending on who's doing the telling. I don't seek to embellish my story, but punk rock made me feel like somebody gave a shit about my story. However, the retelling of real things in history has haunted me my entire life. I love the power of interpretive language.

Zora Neale Hurston had an impact on the way I view language. The poetic nature of her writing combined with the autobiographical nature of her books seemed to spin something that was as much fact as fiction. The rhythm of the way she wrote moved me to no end.

I once saw Sherman Alexie, one of my favorite authors, speak about his writing. He said something like, "this is my bad pile [gesturing with his hands, a very tall stack of paper], and this is my good pile [gesturing to a significantly shorter stack]. This one [the short stack] is full of stuff I got right, and it's a very small amount of paperwork." Writing is about redefining, refining, and trying to make your ideas make sense to someone, or everyone. I always figured that if the lyrics looked good on paper, they were probably good enough for a song.

When I first started writing songs, I didn't have that much life experience. The stories are told and the rhymes are made. Sometimes a song means something, and other times not so much. In retrospect, some of the lyrics in this book are confrontationally juvenile to me. It's okay, but it's a little embarrassing.

The ways people talk, the ways they write, the ebb and flow of the words; it's all so fascinating to me. The rhythm of conversation and the ability to communicate has interested me my whole life. I didn't realize how difficult it was for people, myself in particular, to communicate. Perhaps that's why I started writing songs. Through lyrics and poetry, I found it easier to sum up my feelings. I think I express more about myself in my songs than I do communicating with people close to me.

Whatever it is that I thought I was doing when I first started making rhymes, which I believe was in about second grade, it was apparent that I had a skill. I didn't understand it, but my rhymes always got a response. Sometimes laughter, sometimes approval; either way, it got people's attention. I can only hope that I have lived and learned and become a better writer over time.

I have to mention my high school English teacher, Charlotte Westby. She taught me about poetry in a way that was passionate, and the experience has stayed with me. Other kids thought she was strict and were afraid to take her class, but she made me love language and got me interested in poetry.

I love poetry, and this book is not that. These are lyrics, and if this book is considered close to poetry, I would be okay with that. And I realize some people don't care about what the lyrics are to a song. Some people are more focused on the music. (I actually prefer instrumental music because I get tired of hearing everyone whine about their problems.) Other people have told me they listen only to the lyrics. We all make our own connections to the music we love.

One of my first memories is of scraping a stick along a brick wall: the sound of it, the rhythm of it—it was magic. My childhood experiences were with instrumental music—classical and jazz. As I developed my musical tastes, I began to listen to the lyricists more. Some of my favorite lyricists are Leonard Cohen, Bob Dylan, and Lou Reed, to name just a few. I started reading Dylan Thomas after finding out that Bob Zimmerman changed his last name to Dylan because of him. It's an example of trying to figure out where it all comes from. What's in a gospel song? What are the words? Where did they come from? Why don't we know who wrote certain songs? I can't get these questions out of my head.

I believe it was Leonard Cohen who said, "depression is just the water I swim in." These are the things that go into making a song. You're trying to put out your truth. We joke nowadays about how lonely it is to be a writer. This I know is true.

I suppose the idea for a song could be considered a seed. Some grow to be beautiful plants; others don't germinate at all. They are dormant seeds. No one wants to look at my collection of dormant seeds. They want to see the flower. The big, fat, fucking sunflower. But every seed needs a fair chance. What is it that allows some seeds to turn into flowers? Is it Darwinism? Is it chance? Is it ego? I have no idea. Do I think that my opinion is important? Do I give a shit what anyone thinks? I'm like a dog; I'm peeing on every tree I can find.

songs: dave
dan - "nowhere to go"

karl: bass
drums: pat
dan: guitar - singer
singer - guitar: dave
(dave: sax - "out of style")

thanx: the jizz, moose tone cain.
ambient sound

loud fast rules

WHEN WE FIRST STARTED OUT AS A BAND, WE
needed a name. It was just the three of us, Karl Mueller, Dan Murphy,
and myself. "Loud Fast Rules" seemed like an appropriate name at
the time. I think it came from a photo in a magazine of a guy wearing a
leather jacket that had "Loud Fast Rules" written on the back. It seemed
like a boast, which was cool. Later I changed the name because it felt
like all the music had to fit that description—loud and fast—which was
limiting. The phrase "Soul Asylum" came from some lyrics I wrote. It
wasn't exactly a great song, but it seemed like a great band name.

Now, all these years later, I thought a good way to tie the past and the
present together was to call this collection of songs *Loud Fast Words*.

SOUL ASYLUM

SAY WHAT YOU WILL...

SAY WHAT YOU WILL

I started writing songs that would eventually end up on Soul Asylum's first album, *Say What You Will*, when I was in high school. Back then, I was depressed, going to parties, having a good time, and rockin' out. Doing the stuff every kid does. I quit the hockey team because playing in a band was more important to me.

Loud Fast Rules hit the road around the time I was graduating. At the same time, I was really getting into reading, and the books I was discovering on my own were taking precedence over the books I was assigned in school. I was reading all these books and trying to write all these lyrics, and it became overwhelming. I had two notebooks: my lyric notebook and my homework notebook. I would be studying in a van, trying to decide whether I should work on my lyrics or my homework. I was—wisely or not—always more focused on my lyrics.

When we were out on the road, it started to change the way I looked at the world. People noticed I was doing something different, something that might be interesting to somebody.

The original vinyl version was released in 1984 and included the songs in this chapter. The 1988 rerelease version, *Say What You Will, Clarence,* came out on CD format, and we were able to put the songs that had originally been taken out back onto the record. Those additional songs can be found in the Bonus Tracks & Leftovers chapter.

"LONG DAY"

"Long Day" begins with a character—this alienated, lost person, standing under a streetlight, trying to figure out what to do with their life. Growing up is exhausting, but everything is temporary.

Mine is a lonely one, I forgot to have fun, standing under the streetlight
Ever so nervously, people looking down on me, telling me it's all right

If it were up to me, I'd tear down this whole city, what's all this shit here for?
I give you my heart, but you still say I make you feel like a whore

All this trouble just to die
All this trouble's only temporary
It's temporary

Took away his power, but he hides a tiny flower, in the corner of his jail cell
He's never been outside, he just can't hide, he'd just as soon be in hell

Get off the fucking telephone, why do you hate to be alone
Paranoid of death and love
Ever so patiently, we sit upon our sinking ship, waiting for the black dove

All this trouble just to die
All this trouble's only temporary
It's temporary

I'm sad I couldn't make it, I'm glad that I could fake it, I'm sorry but I got to go
I ain't afraid of cryin', I ain't afraid of dyin', I ain't afraid of things I don't know

Sat around, pulled out my hair, stupid bitches everywhere
No one that can look me in the eye
I ain't afraid of cryin', I ain't afraid of dyin', I ain't afraid of wondering why

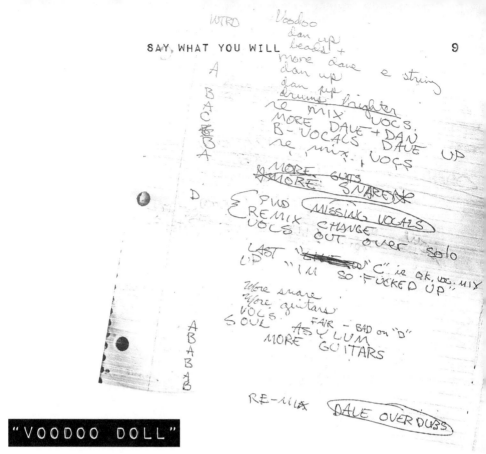

"VOODOO DOLL"

"Voodoo Doll" is about control. Who or what is controlling me? Are we slaves or victims to our obsessions? Or are we just dramatic people? There are also elements of addiction and the idea that "big brother is watching" in this song.

I'm hung up on a wire so thin
Tearing out what's been trapped in
My puppet strings been pulled too tight
Just to see the real me's going to be a bloody fight

I'm your voodoo doll, don't you hear my call?
I'm your voodoo doll, heading for a fall

Trying so hard to forget
Got my bottles, got my pills, got my TV set
I'm imprisoned by my passion, I'm a slave to my trade
How can you be so possessed by the profits that you make?

I love for love where love's insane
I need to numb and ease the pain
When the end begins again
Needles, needles I stick them in

I'm your voodoo doll, don't you hear the call?
I'm your voodoo doll

I'm strung out on pretty, pretty girls
I forgot about the rest of the world
Pots and pans and good free sex, my wife she is the best
If I get bored, I'll get a family and get into incest

I love for love where love's insane
I need to numb and ease the pain
When the end begins again
Needles, needles I stick them in

Your illusions, my confusion
I'm so confused

Think your thoughts, confirm your petty doubts
The spell is cast in broken glass, your time is running out
You're just a prisoner, you're just a prisoner
You're just imprisoned by your own devices
Come on out and bleed some blood
And solve this fucking crisis

I love for love where love's insane
I need to numb and ease the pain
When the end begins again
Needles, needles I stick them in

This world doesn't seem so fucked up when I'm fucked up too

"MONEY TALKS"

I've struggled with other people's materialism and greed for the better part of my life. I find it repulsive to see how money changes people and provokes them to do unimaginable things. It's a bunch of bullshit. This song is inspired by that.

Money talks these days, and everybody listens
We're whipping out our wallets trying to buy what we're missin'
Money screams and says, "I need a slave"
Oh, I'm just trying to find somebody to dig my grave

Everybody's listenin', everybody's listenin', everybody's kissin' a little ass
I said everybody's listenin', all those eyes are glistenin'
All these eyes they say, "Need more, little more, need a little more"

Those corporate kings do crazy things to the mortal man's mind
Machines scream like newborns, artists drop like flies
Well, I'm just tryin' to find somebody to pay my bail
Money screams and says, "My soul is for sale"

Everybody's listenin', everybody's listenin', all those eyes are glistenin'
I said everybody's listenin', every eye is glistenin'
All these eyes

I need a maid to pick up my mess
Help me in the morning, help me get dressed
I'll pay you when I get paid
Well, I'll pay you when I get paid

I'll pay you when I get paid
I'll pay you when I get paid

Money talks these days, and everybody listens
Whatcha gonna do when the burglar says your money or your life?
Money talks these days

"STRANGER"

I wrote "Stranger" in one sitting, and then I played the sax melody. I believe I was coming down from mushrooms at the time. The song was very different from the hardcore punk going on around me. It took a little bit of nerve to be this vulnerable in a song. I was out in the world, hanging out in downtown Minneapolis, and just being an adult for the first time. The punk rock scene in Minneapolis was something I became a part of, and it offered an amazing support system. It's kind of what saved me from feeling like I was going to be suckin' dicks for a dollar. I was invested in the music, but it's scary not knowing if it will ever work out. So, "Stranger" focuses on sentiments I would return to later in my songwriting.

I said, "hey brown girl
I seen your tears through the window
Of the junk shop downtown."
Selling trinkets from your far-off homeland
Did the promise land let you down?
I said, "hey young boy
I notice that you ain't afraid to walk next to me."
"Old man, you look like you're dying
Is that all you want, is a quarter from me?"

Sometimes I feel like a stranger
Then I feel even stranger

I'm just another face in a faceless crowd
I'm just another king in a headless crown
I'm so alone
You know I live here in this city
But this place, it just ain't nobody's home
Now how many times do I got to tell you?
There's no such thing as a man-made world

How many times do I got to tell you?
There's no such thing as a man-tamed girl

Sometimes I feel like a stranger
Then I feel even stranger

I want to buy some flowers for my mother
If I only had another chance
You see, I got a happy family
But that's oh so far away
You see, I've got it all here inside me
But I just can't seem to get it out
But I know, with a little imagination
We can work this whole goddamn thing out

Don't make me feel like a stranger

"SICK OF THAT SONG"

"Sick of That Song" is a reaction to all the music we heard on the radio that we thought was shit. All the lyrical content of those songs seemed exactly the same. I suppose there's a bit of irony overdose here. The song is pretty smart-ass.

I'm sick of that song about how you lost your lover
I'm sick of that song about how you treat your mother
I'm sick of that song about your useless solutions

I'm sick of that song

I'm sick of that song about how you look at life
And I'm sick of that song about how you treat your wife
I'm sick of that song about your sha-na-blah-blah

I'm sick of that song

I'm sick of that song about sex, drugs, and rock
I'm sick of that song about how you love your cock
I'm sick of that song about your bitching bad luck
And all those women you fuck

I'm sick of that song
I'm sick of that song
I'm sick of that song
I'm sick of that song

"WALKING"

The bass line in "Walking" is based on a marimbula I heard in Jamaica. This song is about the beginning of finding out what else is out there, feeling like I must be making some sort of progress to a destination, and I am getting closer.

The sun's creeping up and stomping on my dreams
Works all right, partying's fine
But sleeping is my scene

The traffic inside your head is tearing you apart
So, stick your fingers down my throat
And grab onto my heart

And I'm walking a little closer
Walkin' a little closer
Walkin' a little closer

Gonna rise up, take you away
Sunday's just another day

The only thing I can guarantee
If you cut me, I will bleed

Her eyes shine like oceans
And her skin is like the earth
Suck the life out of her
You better take her for what she's worth

No free ride, yeah, this bus is going charter
So, get up off your ass, come on try just a little harder

Try a little harder
Try a little harder

And I'm walking a little closer
Walkin' just a little closer
Walkin' a little closer

Yeah, your one-track bible history
Will never solve this mystery

Don't want your money, don't want your land
I just want you to understand
Come on take that step
Take that step
Walk these walls of ignorance

Fall in, fall in, how desperate are we?

I'm walking a little closer
Just walkin' a little closer
I'm walkin' a little closer

"HAPPY"

"Happy" is the early pinnacle of my cynicism and sarcasm. I thought it was interesting to express the opposite of how I felt. I don't know if anyone got it.

When I'm with my friends, my troubles end
When I'm with the boys, I don't hear your noise
When we're together, it could last forever
And I'm almost there
I'm almost there

I'm away from the boss, at least for awhile
I'm away from the girls that cramp my style

I'm away from the works, I'm away from the jerks
And I'm almost there, I'm almost there

It's happy time

I'll take four of those, and couple of those
And more of those, and more of those

I'm away from the works, I'm away from the jerks
And I'm almost there, I'm almost there

Happy time

Everybody's so happy

I'm not gonna wait around
So fuck this silly life
Build a fire and pitch a tent
And tell me it's all right

Let's wreck this wall
I'm away from it all
And I'm almost there
I'm almost there

Everybody is so happy

WALKING

VOC. RE-DUE
MIX IS ALRIGHT
~~LITTLE MORE BASS~~?

MORE DAVE "TRY HARDER"

GUITARS AT END ARE COOL

TAKE 2

VOODOO
MORE DAVE + DAN
MORE SNAP ON SNARE
DAVE OVERDUBS
RE-MIX VOCS
HIGH PARTS DAVE?
MORE CRASH

SOUL ASYLUM
MORE DAVE GUITARS
RE-DUE OR VOCS. or 2
TOO MUCH KICK

SPACE HEAD
MORE DAVE + DAN
TOO MUCH KICK
RE-DUE VOCS. — LOW "SPACE HEAD"
MORE CRASH

MASQURADE
MORE VERB ON SAX - 2nd SAX
RE-DUE VOCS.
MORE DAN
RE-MIX END COMPRESS

BACK + BLU
INTRO

A   UP COP. BEAT
IS   BRIGHTER DAVE RYTHEM
A   LESS HIGH HAT
     MORE GUITAR TOO MUCH
     RE-DO VOCS.
TAKE EFFECTS OFF
     SOLO AND REST

MORE CRASH
BRIGHTER OR SNARE

RELIGIVISION
MUSHY BASS
COOL INTRO   OUT VOC.
BUILD INTO VOCS IN MIX

MORE DAVE SOLO
MORE B. VOCS.

A
B   TRY TWO IS BETTER MIXED
C   OTHER VOC. TRACK
           or RE-DO
     SOUNDS. STUFF IS CUTTING OUT

     BREAK
     RE-MIX MORE of everything
     CLIMAX IS BULL SHIT VOCS.
     MORE DAN
     MORE CRASH
A
B
C   PER-HAP MIX IN INTERESTING VOC

4

BLACK + BLUE
TOO MANY EFFECT STUFFS
UP AH - AH - AAH
SOUNDS MUSHY + WIMPY
MORE SHARPNESS

HOW IS   HEAR OLD COPY

YOUR   RELIGIVISION
         VOCALS TOO LOUD
MAMA   MORE SNARE
         MORE CLEAN ~~BASE~~ BASS
DOING?   DO YOU KNOW
         INTERESTING HARMO VOCS
         BRAGGING

RE-DO VOCS

WALKING
FUK DAYS B-VOCS
8

Bait the Bitch
Take my Jizz
Drive me through the truck
Twist my ...
Kick me ...

"BLACK AND BLUE"

I wrote "Black and Blue" right after the first time Soul Asylum ever played in public as a band. The cops came in, shut down the show, and made everyone leave. Being shut down by the cops is a normal thing when you're playing in basements and warehouses and house parties. And sometimes the cops were really not cool. It made me angry because I thought they should have better things to do.

Protect and serve, slice my nerve
Gotta make sure everybody's gonna get what they deserve

Make my plea, I'm down on my knees
Street cowboy with a badge that says you can do what you please
Do what you please, do what you please

Rape me, take me, shine your lights so I can't see
Holsters, guns, and uniforms
Just don't impress me

Bloodstained streets, he looks pretty neat
Somebody's cryin' for help, he's breaking up my party

Please stop breathing down my neck
Took away something that's mine, I want you to give it back
You gotta give it back, now give it back

Walk across my face with your shiny shoes
Bow down to the badge
And colors black and blue

The blue night, he rides tonight
It's your street, it's a powerless fight
So just take me home, 'cause I'm not alone
Just take me home, I'm not alone

The squads breakin' down
But you misjudged power
So get your handcuffs ready
'Cause we're coming in numbers

"RELIGIAVISION"

Television in the early and mid-eighties seemed to be experiencing an influx of evangelical programing. Growing up in the Catholic Church made these hucksters on television seem sleazy and crass to me. Watching them actually offended my sense of spirituality at the time. Everyone's just trying to get your money. Amen.

Nail myself up way up high and I'm'a gonna die for you
Mother offers up her child to the preachings of channel two

The empires rise and the babies cry, when is the lesson going to be learned?
And all I hear is the commercials and now the crosses are gonna burn

Crosses are gonna burn

I like to watch religious TV, what you get is not what you see
What you get is not what you see
Not what you see

What you get is not what you see
Not what you see

Oh god, that's enough, that's enough, that's enough

Religiavision

Now I ain't gonna be the one to wash away your sins
Why do the children have to pay for the poor planning that you did?

No matter how loud I scream and cry, you're gonna be sentenced to suffer
You married your life and you married your wife
Now you're gonna have to learn to love her
Can you really love her?

Can you really love her?

I like to watch religious TV, what you get is not what you see
What you get is not what you see
Not what I see

What you get is not what you see
Not what you see

Religiavision

Save me, my dear fucking Lord, won't you please take my hand?
Lead me to your sweet salvation in McDonaldland

I was born a wild and beautiful baby, but you tried to tell me what to be
Can you love your children knowing you must set them free?

You must set them free

I like to watch religious TV, what you get is not what you see
What you get is not what you see
Not what I see

What you get is not what you see

Religiavision

Would you feel it in your heart if I sacrificed my life?

SOUL ASYLUM

MADE TO BE BROKEN

MADE TO BE BROKEN

During the making of *Made to Be Broken*, I had already dropped out of college and I was working at Tracy's Saloon and Hennepin Lake Liquors. The band was on the road constantly. We were fucking gone all the time. It seemed like it was three hundred shows a year. How we managed to get into the studio and put out two full-length albums in one year is amazing considering how much time we were spending on the road. I guess we had the freedom to do whatever the fuck we wanted to do. There was no "is this the right kind of song, for the right kind of record?" There was none of that. Twin/Tone Records allowed us to record whatever we wanted.

So, we went back into the studio with Bob Mould. He had produced the first record as well. What's hilarious to me is, this was kind of our "comeback record" after our drummer quit. Pat Morley, who played on the first record, quit the band to go into treatment, and I thought it was all over. I thought we were done. I was literally crying about it. I remember saying to Dan Murphy, "we can't let this [the band] go, but I don't know how we can go on." It was the first of many times I've had that conversation.

Then, I met Grant Young at this house where these MCAD students lived. I was mostly there to hang out with Mike Etoll, who is more or less a cultural fixture in Minneapolis. Mike and I were playing tiddlywinks in the basement, and I heard Grant practicing drums upstairs, and I asked him to join the band.

We went into the studio and cut "Tied to the Tracks," Dan's song "Long Way Home," and "It's Alright, Ma," a Bob Dylan cover. I was still finding my legs, and I didn't know if anybody wanted to hear my songs. Then Bob Mould said something like, "What the fuck? No one wants to hear you cover Bob Dylan. They want to hear your songs."

This all snowballed into the record that is *Made to Be Broken*. I guess we were on a roll. I was writing a lot, all the time. I used to demand it out of myself that I just fill up notebooks constantly. It didn't even matter what I was writing; I just had to be writing, pretty much at all times.

"TIED TO THE TRACKS"

I remember watching cartoons as a kid, and it seemed like there was always someone tying someone else to the railroad tracks. It's hilarious to me to think that the train is never actually coming. "Tied to the Tracks" has a sentiment of impatience, of wanting your life to go somewhere and feeling held back. But it's just me holding myself back. The only person who can untie me from the tracks is me.

What are you doing here in my nightmare?
Stepping back into the stupid years gets me nowhere

Look at you now
You look like an angel in hell
Look at you now
Drowning in your wishing well
Look at you now
Hard-luck stories and there's no one to tell
Look at you now

Do you think you can find a place for your dreams in my nightmare?
And you're tied to the tracks, but the train's broke down
Wake me up and let me go
You're somebody I used to know from somewhere in my nightmare
Don't you remember the years we got nowhere?

Look at you now
You look like an angel in hell
Look at you now
Drowning in your wishing well
Look at you now
Hard-luck stories and there's no one to tell
Look at you now

Do you think you can find a place for your dreams in my nightmares?
And you're playing with a different joker; there's always one more sucker
And you're tied to the tracks, but the train's broke down
Strapped at the top of a merry-go-round, but it won't let you down

Look at you now
You look like an angel in hell
Look at you now
Drowning in your wishing well
Look at you now
Hard-luck stories and there's no one to tell
Look at you now

Do you think you could find a place for your dreams?

"SHIP OF FOOLS"

I remember when I was trying to sort out the lyric sheet for "Ship of Fools," the culture and the times were crazy. I mean, we were living in a van and on the road all the time. We were getting out there and getting into it. "Ship of Fools" was about all the dumbshits you run into at bars, and how everyone wants to start a fight. It was ridiculous. I knew I was going to be playing in bars for the rest of my life, so I thought I better get used to it.

We were shipwrecked sailors searching for some fool's gold
They were the drunken local boys
We'd been out drinking all night and feeling all right
We watched them kill each other in a fight

Ship of fools, drunken hearts
Making yet another new start
Ain't it hard to play that part?
When you've got a drunken heart?

Well, I can't change the world by complaining
You can't change it with a kiss
There'd be no concentrating, contemplating
No time to find out what we missed

Ship of fools, drunken hearts
Making yet another new start
Ain't it hard to play that part?
When you've got a drunken heart?

"ANOTHER WORLD, ANOTHER DAY"

"Another World, Another Day" experiments with time signatures, which ultimately affects the meter of the lyric.

The line "On the day you walked away" is another meditation on coming out of your shell or leaving where you came from and going out into the world and exploring.

Folks tell jokes in clouds of smoke
Making sure life won't decay
Fancy flags fly in your face
Fall polluting in my space

Pounds of sounds from shotgun rounds
Music of the hit parade
Now your father's, father's, father's
He's got nothing left to say
On the day you walked away

Another world, another day

"MADE TO BE BROKEN"

"Made to Be Broken" is where country music comes in. We're from Minnesota, where there's lots of country farmland, and we're exposed to country music at a very young age, whether we like it or not. You could hear the influence of country music on some punk bands of the day; I think they called it "cow punk." That's sort of where I was going with this one. It's like a two-step, and we're playing it as fast as we can.

Country music, jazz music, punk music—you can label it however you want; I love it all. I believe cow punk is now commonly referred to as "Americana." Silly semantics.

Yes, I'll be leaving in the morning
By the chill that you gave me I will ride
I will tear out my insides just to find a place to hide
And I don't wanna hurt you anymore

You got the dagger, but I got the revolver
As we rolled and we tumbled to the floor
I've been shot upside the ceiling
Is it just these drugs I'm feeling?
And I don't wanna lie to you no more

Now this advice I will lend
To spend until the end
A guitar's a man's best friend
And these rules were made to be broken

I'm not trying to make myself uneasy
And I haven't got the guts to make you cry
Someone's tellin' me one thing,
Lord knows we've got to do something
And I don't want to hurt you anymore

Now this advice I will lend
To spend until the end
Some things aren't meant to be spoken
And these rules are made to be broken
Made to be broken, made to be broken, made to be

"NEVER REALLY BEEN"

"Never Really Been" is entrenched in growing up in Minnesota. It's also where I started to dig deep into music that I had not yet really explored.

My girlfriend at the time worked at a jazz bar in Minneapolis called the Artists' Quarter. I fucking loved that place. I would go pick her up from work, and I would watch the jazz performers until she got done. It consolidated my whole love for music and, in particular, jazz music.

I wrote this song around the time our drummer, Pat Morley, quit the band. I was lost and young, and I didn't know what to do with my life. After I got the news about Pat, I was walking home from the Artists' Quarter on a beautiful, quiet, snowy night in Minneapolis. I wrote about the "sound of snow falling down"—which is silence.

Sirens are screaming, shots ring out at night
Movie cameras rolling in
And there goes my hero with his head between his legs
And all this time I believed in him

Now what is the sound of snow falling down
On the tombstone in the dead of the night?
And who is the hound at the downtown dog pound
Who speaks English when the watchman's not in sight?

And where will you be in 1993?
Still sitting in the same chair?
Sinning is for sinners and I'm just a beginner
But I've never really been punched there

Hey, ain't it strange how some things never change
Ain't it strange how nothing stays the same
You were thinkin' I was distressed about some universal press
But I was just depressed about my last pinball game

I've learned to accept, and not to expect
The respect and neglect that I get
I've tried not to forget about what hasn't happened yet
And on this, I place my last bet

Did you give what you get
Did you get what you give
Of your fair share wear and tear?
Winning is for winners
And I know spring follows winter
But I've never really been touched there

You know it's hard to be nice
When hate becomes your vice
And you can't find peace anywhere
Love's not just for lovers
Get off your high horse, brother
Drop your fists and get out of here.

5½ ITs hard to be nice when hate becomes your vice
and you cant find peace anywhere.
loves not just for lovers, drop your cove
don't stand and stare, just take me their

1 What is the sound of snow falling down
on a tombstone in the dead of the night.
Who is the hound at the down town dog pound
who speaks england when his owners not in sight
and where will you be in 1993 still sitting in
the same chair
Sinning is for sinners, and I'm just a begginer
but I've never really been punched their

2 Sirens a screamin shots ring out the night
movie cameras roling in
their goes my hero with his head between his
legs, and all this time I believed in him
Spaceship doin 800 cars down 55 those who walk + drive tank
feel no shame

"WHOA!"

I had been trying so hard to express myself and I had found my avenue. I realized the cathartic nature of hardcore punk rock was a good way to direct my rage. "Whoa!" is not so much about the words; it's more about screaming bloody murder. Because I can't express myself, it feels good to just fucking scream sometimes.

Whoa!

I want love, love right now, someway somehow
I'm desperate for a buzz

Whoa!

X, express, expression, someway somehow
I'm desperate for a buzz

Whoa!

Life's my life, life's my right, my right, right now

Whoa!
I said whoa!

"NEW FEELINGS"

"New Feelings" is a song about self-discovery and getting over your hang-ups and moving on.

Roll away the chain that wraps around me
Wipe the spider webs from my eyes
Tumble down the tall walls that surround me
It's my time, no lies, no alibis

New feelings

Now my daydreams just don't seem so far away

No, I'm not possessed by my possessions
If I had to clear my right to die
You're in love with your evangelist investment
In my time, I don't need an alibi

New feelings

Now my daydreams just don't seem so far away

My head's like a wrecking ball and you look like a wall
Mopping up the tears that fill your eyes
This is my life, my right, and that's not all
I just laughed my head right off and cried

New feelings

Now my daydreams just don't seem so far away

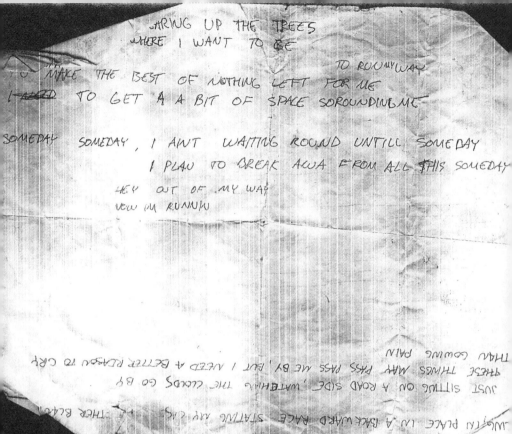

"GROWING PAIN"

When I was very young, I would get an ache or a pain, and I didn't know what it was. My mom or dad would tell me it was a growing pain. It got me wondering, is the emotional part of growing up worse than the physical pain? You think your leg hurts, well, try having your heart broken. How do you like that?

Riding into town when the sun goes down
And the natives get restless and the crowd comes 'round
Pacin' in place in a backwards race
While statin' my case to another blank face

I'm just sitting on the roadside
Watching all the cars and the clouds roll by
They may pass me by
But I need a better reason to cry

Growing pain, it leaves a stain
That's similar, but not the same
It's down the drain and what remains
Maybe you're the one who's a little insane

Now everything's lovely if you're ugly
What you would, what you should, and what you could be
Mister Right spends his life stabbing himself with a butter knife

I'm just sitting on the roadside
Watching all the cars and the clouds roll by
They may pass me by
But I need a better reason to cry

Growing pains, a spinning blade
Whirling 'round, you're like a razor-edged chain
It's down the drain and what remains
Maybe you're the one who's a little insane

Growing pain, it leaves a stain
It's similar, but not the same
It's down the drain and what remains
Maybe you're the one who can make that change

Can't shake hands with boxing gloves
With whips and chains, you'll never make love

"LONE RIDER"

"Lone Rider" is a testament to independence. That's how I roll. I'm the lone rider, and I don't need fucking anybody. I'm a lonely dude, on a lonely planet. It sounds overdramatic, but I was young.

Peeping Tom creepin' through the mornin' moonlight
Like a crazy coyote in the middle of the night
You keep taggin' along until it does you wrong
Sometimes it takes so long for you to say, "so long"

Not for the lone rider

Black clouds troll wherever he goes
He breaks out in a cold sweat when you get too close
Your suitcase is home, long may you roam, lone rider
Ohh, baby's cryin', please come home lone rider

Your reflection's in the water, but the water's a mirage
It's like a dream machine that never leaves the garage
Your boots start walkin', as the story goes
People start talkin' and the restlessness grows

They say he hates people; they say he's a queer
Never listens, but always hears
Off into the sunset he disappears
Surely the last time to come around here

Ride on lone rider

"AIN'T THAT TOUGH"

I thought "Ain't That Tough" was a good double entendre to meditate on.
I'm not a fighter; I'm a lover. So, am I saying that you "ain't that tough,"
or that your life "ain't that tough"?

A sweet scent of discontent rising in the air
You don't get old, you just get passive
And then you stand and stare

Hey, nobody's keeping you from stopping

Like a plug without a socket
Your finger trigger's itching
But you forgot to cock it

And now, things didn't turn out the way you thought they would be
No, you can't take that out on me
If you can find a better way, then I ain't standing in your way

I'm fed up with holding out
I called your bluff, now let it out
You were thinking it was never enough
It ain't bad luck, it's just that you ain't that tough

Ain't that tough

A graveyard of bottles and a throttle pointing for your lips
If you're so brave why's a .45 hang from your hips?
No, nobody's keeping you from stopping
You're always threatening to kill yourself
Well, why don't you just do it right here, right now?

I didn't turn out the way you thought I would be
No, you can't take that out on me
I thought I was talking to someone else
I guess I was talking to myself

I'm fed up with holding out
I called your bluff, now let it out
You were thinking it was never enough
It ain't bad luck, it's just you ain't that tough

Last time I talked to you, you talked just like me
Now you're talking like some Hollywood actress
Hey, what the hell's that supposed to mean?

Last time I talked to you
You turned and walked away

What the fuck

You ain't that tough

"DON'T IT (MAKE YOUR TROUBLES SEEM SMALL)"

"Don't It (Make Your Troubles Seem Small)" is a good finish to the album because after all the punk rock bitching and moaning, it's good to get some perspective. Think about how much better off you are than a lot of other people. Don't it make your troubles seem small?

You're talking like another mouth to feed
Shopping for things that you don't need
Smile child, you'll only be wild for a while

Fall, waterfall
Dig my grave anytime at all
My friend punched another hole into the wall

Don't it make your troubles seem small?

You're moaning and you're groaning
Everybody around you just makes you lonely
I'm just trying to get to you, before you get to me

Fall, waterfall
Dig my grave anywhere at all
Cockroaches crawling up my wall

Don't it make your troubles seem small?

WHILE YOU WERE OUT

A s we were working on our third album, we couldn't decide what to call it. I wanted to call it *Malice in Wonderland* because I thought that was hilarious. I sadly discovered that Nazareth had already used the name, for fuck's sake. So, the name we ended up with for the record came from those notepads they used to have in offices to take messages on that said, "While you were out."

At this point we were part of a family that was operating out of a space at Twenty-Sixth Street and Nicollet Avenue in Minneapolis. Twin/Tone Records and Hüsker Dü both had their offices upstairs in the building, and the studio was in the back. Paul Stark was the ringleader of Twin/Tone. They called him "Fish Finder," but I never understood why; maybe it was because he was always trying to get a fish tank to work properly in the office.

The atmosphere was glorious. Twin/Tone and Hüsker Dü and the people who were running the studio, especially Roz at the front desk—they were amazing. Dave Ayers was our manager, and I would see him and Peter Jesperson and Abbie Kane and all these people every day, because we also practiced in the back of the building. And then, voilà, Twin/Tone hired my guitar mentor, Chris Osgood of the Suicide Commandos. I love Chris. If you're trying to figure out who's cool and who are your favorite local musicians, I picked the right guy for that. I mean, Chris is super smart and really funny. So, it was a no-brainer to hire him to produce *While You Were Out*. It was a dream come true.

"FREAKS"

At the time we were writing the songs for While You Were Out, *I lived in a small apartment with three other people. I was so proud of the lyrics I had written for "Freaks" that I put them up on the bathroom wall. I believe it was six sheets of paper. The general reaction among my roommates was, "Is there something wrong with Dave?" I suppose the song is an anthem for individuality. What makes you different, or why people make fun of you, is what makes you beautiful. Those were strange times.*

Made your killing
Guts start spilling
Here's a piece of a puzzle
Piece of your trouble
Piece of somethin' else
Yourself, myself

But I'm so untamed, without a clue
Think I can find something better
Something better to do

I should be so excited
I'm into something new
Could be some new kind of old thing
Could be just something to use

Maybe I should practice it one more time
Maybe I'm afraid what it might do
Maybe it might upset someone
Maybe that's what it's supposed to do
You've put up quite a lot of resistance to change
But with another existence, that's what you're trying to say

I'm not pushing you out
I'm not pushing you off
I'm not pushing you out
I'm pushing you onto the next panel of experts
To tell you what to do
And you come back to the next panel of experts
Experts like me and you

Look what you've done to me
Look what I've done to you
Look what they've done to us
Now we're like no one else

They're laughing at you
Talking about you
All these new things
All these new things
I bought them used

And I'm working so hard on what I'm thinking is real
Everybody dies once just to see how it feels
It's not a sensation, and it's not for sale
So, what can you call it now?

Have you forgotten?
Let it spoil you rotten
Have you forgotten?
Have you forgotten?
You're just another freak
A beautiful freak
We are freaks

"CARRY ON"

Although the band had graduated from such behavior by this time, when we were younger and struggling, we would go to blood banks and then go immediately across the street with our checks to the liquor store to buy beer. It seemed hilarious, fun, and fucked up all at the same time. I was just trying to get through it. In "Carry On," I'm sort of complaining and saying it's worth it, however much beer and blood it takes. "Things will be better, because they can't get much worse."

This will be over
I hope you don't mind the pain
I wanna cut you
And let the poison all drain
Give me a shot quick
I think I know how this works
Things will be better
Because they can't get much worse

And we will carry on
Carry on

Now, I can't carry the weight of your hang-ups
They're dead weight, they're made out of lead
And I can't carry the guilt or frustration
Of something someone else said

Now I'm just learning to carry myself
Carry myself on my own
I'm just looking to carry myself
Carry on, carry on, carry on

Whenever I see you
I know you think I don't know
That I can't be you
You think your thoughts they don't show
I want to trust you
I want to trust you so bad
I want to bust you
Stealing the few things we had

And we will carry on
Carry on

Now's the place to lose your fate
Keep the faith that reinstates
The habits that are forming what you feel

This will be over

"NO MAN'S LAND"

"No Man's Land" was an important song to me because it addresses the taking of Native American land. I often come back to issues like this in my writing. It's really important to me. The concept of claiming a piece of land is a little ridiculous, and pretty white.

In a town without a name
There is no shame, no fame to claim
One fine day the pilgrims came
And made new rules for an old game

And I'm waiting for the garbage man to take you away
And I'm searching for my playground so I can go and play

So they built a big smokestack
They built a railroad track, they paved the dirt roads black
And they did it behind your back
And now you pay their tax, hoping something cracks

And I'm waiting for the garbage man to take you away
And I'm searching for my playground so I can go and play

From out of the dust came corrosion and rust
That made your lust so cheap
There's nothing to have here and nothing to hold here
And nothing that you can keep

Understand this is no man's land
And it's all that's left that's free
Where the kings of nothing rule, my friend
And you can't make me leave

There's a billboard in the sky
Reflecting water in your eyes
This big city, this ghost town
Will come crumbling to the ground

And I'm waiting for the hurricane to blow you away
And I'm searching for my twister to twist you into shape

Now my speech is said and done
The circus came, I've had my fun
And the wasteland has been won
And the building has begun

And I'm waiting for the earthquake to shake you down
And I see my mother nature coming to slap you around

IN A TOWN WITHOUT A NAME
NO FAME TO CLAIM
THERE IS NO SHAME
THEN ON DAY THE PILGRIMS CAME
AND MADE NEW RULES FOR AN
OLD GAME
and I'm waiting for the caretaker man to
take you away
and I'm looking for a playground
so I can go and play
SO THEY BUILT THEY BUILT THE BIG SMOKE STACKS
THEY PAVED PAVED THER DIRT ROADS BLACK
THEY LAID A RAILROAD TRACK
THEY DID IT ALL BIHIND OUR BACK
NOT EVEN THEY CAN GIVE IT BACK

AND OUT OF THE DUST
CAME A SERIOUS LUST

"THE JUDGE"

Somebody has to judge the judge. I mean, why is everyone judging each other all day long? Whether it's a traffic violation that you have to go down to city hall and sort out or it's your mother telling you why your next-door neighbor is a creep, I just don't get why people are so quick to judge each other. At some point, I began to believe that judgment should be one of the seven deadly sins.

I see you passing judgment
It ain't judgment day
I can't let you misjudge me that way

Ain't shooting for perfection
I'm scared of my reflection
But I can't let you misjudge me that way

I used to think that I could raise myself above it
You can make me break down and cry
But you can't make me love it

And I can't fake it, you can't take it
I ain't holding no grudge
'Cause I can't judge it, and you can't judge it
And who's gonna judge the judge?
Who's gonna judge the judge?

High falootin' aloofin'
Has got you in its ways
I can't let you misjudge me that way

Not that I care what you think of me
But I hear every word that you say
And I can't let you misjudge me that way

Sticks and stones may break my bones
But I can't take the blame
You can find yourself a new scapegoat
But I won't play the game

I can't make it, you can't take it
I ain't holding no grudge
'Cause I can't judge it, and you can't judge it
And who's gonna judge the judge?
Who's gonna judge the judge?

What did you do?
You look pretty guilty

I see you pointing fingers
You're pointing one my way
I can't let you misjudge me that way

I never said I was innocent
But I just might have something to say
And I can't let you misjudge me that way

No, I can't let you misjudge me that way

"SUN DON'T SHINE"

The double meaning is so solid in "Sun Don't Shine." I always had to put up with the expression, "I'm going to put that hockey puck where the sun don't shine." The song is about exploring the darkness while trying to find the light, with a little bit of "stick it up your ass" in there as well. It's much too deep.

Picture if you will a house on the hill
Where the family kills each other for a place in the will
Understand if you can a dirty old man
Who holds a plastic rosary in the palm of his hand

And under the rug you will sweep
Secrets and promises you can't keep
The dam it will leak, it will weep
Said, "I'd like to tell you how I feel"
You said, "You know that can't be real, it's much too deep"

Why'd you wanna watch and wait, you can't walk on water
Get your feet on the ground
There's a hole in the floor, hole in the door
Whole wide world waiting to turn you around

And under the rug you will sweep
Secrets and promises you can't keep
The dam it will leak, it will weep
Said, "I'd like to tell you how I feel"
You said, "You know that can't be real, it's much too deep"

Now how will you keep yourself busy?
Take the trouble you're leaving behind
And dig down deep where you do not belong
Then shine a light where the sun doesn't shine

Seven days, still no sign of daylight
Your tunnel's collapsing from behind
And how the hell did I get to Alaska?
Shine a light where the sun doesn't shine

"CLOSER TO THE STARS"

I'm embracing metaphor in this song. There are so many ways you can use star—it's just a great word. So, there are metaphors here about heaven, the cosmos, movie stars, caterpillars turning into butterflies, and so on. And I guess the song is wrapped up in questions about what it is that people think they want.

Caterpillar crawling up the big phone pole
Is there somebody that you want to talk to?
You know that pretty soon, you'll be able to fly
How is this going to affect you?
Do you think it might wreck you?
Your friends might reject you
Say you took it too far
They'll say you want to be, want to be, wanna be, want to be

Hooked on glossy pictures and drugs I've never seen
Treat you with advice from a fashion magazine
One day she just walked into that magazine
I wonder if she'll ever come back
And they all said she would crack
They said her mind was one-track
Said she took it too far
They said you want to be, want to be, wanna be, want to be
Closer to the stars

Every time you move your lips
Let me give you a few tips
Yesterday you were too young
Tomorrow you will be too old to regret all the things you've done

Who're you trying to hustle?
Somebody you want to show your muscles
Secondhand excuses never went too far
What's this scene you're making?
Your ideas have been taken
Sick when you are waking, alone in someone's car
You just stood there shaking, you stood there shaking
They said you were faking
They said you want to be, want to be, wanna be, want to be
Closer to the stars

"NEVER TOO SOON"

The expression "life is what happens to you while you're busy making other plans" comes to mind with this song. "Never Too Soon" is a call to action and an anthem against laziness. You get the idea; whatever it is you're thinking about doing all day, just go do it. It's never too late to become an artist, or whatever it is you want to be, so get to it, because it's never too soon.

Now you're bad; you're leaving home
'Cause you say there's no one there for you to talk to
Isn't it nice to go outside
When you know there is no place you have to walk to
You could live alone inside a crowded room
Consume or you'll be consumed
And it's never, never too late, never too soon

Put on your frown and go downtown
Where you wait in line to find your mind is blown
You have come a long, long way
Even though you had no idea where you're going
You ain't done a goddamn thing all afternoon
Your confidence is sinking like a lead balloon
It's never, never too late, never too soon

I can't calm down, I can't come down
I can't come down, I can't calm down
I can't grow up, I can't give up
It's not your fault and it's not mine
It's not like I'm asking you to hold up the sky

All the things you held so high
Are you surprised to find that now they add to nothing?
Now you're growing old and bold
Do you think that maybe you could teach me something?

There is nothing that you really can assume
But you could be the wallflower in someone's room
And it's never, never too late, never too soon

Now you're mad, I know you're mad
Now you're mad, I know you're mad
Why don't you just tell someone
It's not like you're the only one
It's not like I'm asking you to hold up the sky

I can teach you how to try
You can teach me how to lie
Hush my darling, don't you cry
This could be your lullaby
Never, never too late

"LAP OF LUXURY"

"Lap of Luxury" is kind of a joke. It's talking about how life would be easier with more money. When I was a kid, there was a side to heavy metal music where guys would brag about how much money they were making. I did not see that coming with the hip-hop genre, bragging about money. But as the Notorious B.I.G. once said, "mo' money, mo' problems." I had no idea what having money meant when I wrote this song. I was just making fun of everything.

I ain't working nine to five
I ain't going out to plant no seed
I don't ask what I'm supposed to do
'Cause I've got everything I want
But I don't have anything I need

Well, I do my thing in a palace full of kings
Do it in an old broken-down shack
I'd give you the shirt off my back
Show you where your systems lack
Meet you in the lap of luxury

I get off the floor and walk it off
Get back to a place where I can see
I'm coming back for more abuse
Meet you in the lap of luxury

Now I'm working noon to midnight
Now my precious seeds they have been sown
I don't ask when they're supposed to grow
'Cause I got everything I know
I don't know anything I need

No exploitation, paid vacation
All I want's communication
That ain't too hard to see
When the van stops rolling, the band starts rocking
It ain't too pretty, it ain't too shocking
But I've got everything I need

I get off the floor and walk it off
Get back to a place where I can see
I'm coming back for more abuse
Meet you in the lap of luxury

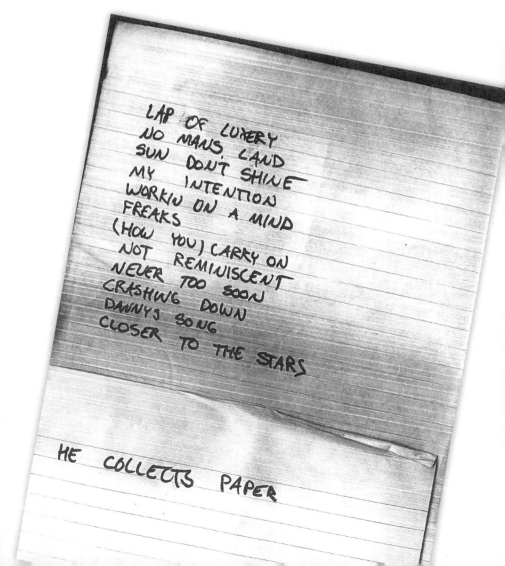

"PASSING SAD DAYDREAM"

You could call "Passing Sad Daydream" a country-blues meditation. It's very long, it's very slow, and it's relentless in its sense of irony and pissing in the face of whatever music aesthetic the band was supposed to be. My instinct was always to go in the opposite direction from that. Funny enough, we were playing the song at CBGB in New York and an A&R guy from A&M Records was there. He later said, "When I heard 'Passing Sad Daydream,' I decided to sign you to my record label." Hilarious.

If you're walking home late at night
Dressed up and alone
Don't you get tired of being white where buffalo never roam?

Going to sneak up behind you
Steal your thoughts, tap your phone
'Cause you might be keeping secrets that you ain't supposed to know

Now it's a fine-tuned machine
And you must feed it more
And the lovely Miss Liberty is just another whore

It's hard to see things your way
It's hard to understand; hard to understand the things you say
But most of all, it's hard to get high these days

If you've got to hate someone
You might as well hate yourself
You'll find that you don't deserve it more than anyone else

So, get out of your kitchen
And get out of your bed
Got to tell them what you've always wanted to tell them
'Cause in the morning you might be dead

So, don't call the doctor
'Cause I'll be okay
It's just a passing sad daydream that led me astray

And it's hard to see things your way
And it's hard to understand, it's hard to understand the things you say
But most of all, it's hard to get high these days

And I ain't proud of nothing
But it's better that way
'Cause it's too loud for talking, and there ain't much to say

So, pack up your explosives
And pack up your gun
'Cause if you ain't chasing someone, you've got to be on the run

And I'm so far from home now
There's nothin' there anyway
I ain't lookin' to make a living, I just need a place to stay

CLAM DIP
AND OTHER DELIGHTS

Whip Cream and Other Delights, by Herb Alpert's Tijuana Brass, was the filthiest record cover in everyone's parents' collection. That album was released by A&M Records, and since A&M was interested in Soul Asylum, we took the opportunity to spoof the Herb Alpert cover. That's our MO: we can't take things too seriously, so we just make fun of everything.

We recorded the six-song EP Clam Dip and Other Delights during the grace period between Twin/Tone and A&M. Since we were swimming between labels, we made a European version and released it with three different covers. By the time it came out in America we had signed with A&M, and the Alpert-inspired version with bassist Karl Mueller half-naked sitting in a mound of clam dip and dead fish is what stuck as the album cover. It also stunk. It was a bit of a lark.

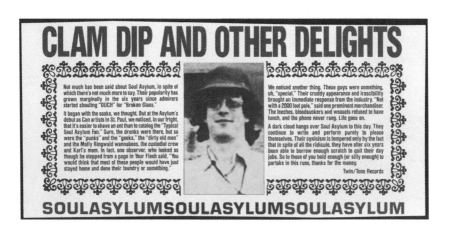

"JUST PLAIN EVIL"

*I don't put a lot of stock in the devil, but it seems like a thriving enterprise.
Sometimes people are just bad, and there's really no excuse for being an
asshole.*

You sold your soul for a lump of coal
Blacker than the night
Didn't think you'd be needing it
'Cause you thought you were brought up right

But you never know who you might meet
On the street where the church bells ring to a different beat

Is it joy, is it pain?
Is it rusted in the rain?
Do you really think I need it?
Is it just plain evil?

Heard of a man who had a plan
To save the wretched world
Nationwide genocide
To save the boys and girls

Like one-eyed jacks and suicide kings
Look out for beady eyes I think
You know what I mean?

Is it good, is it bad?
Is it bitter, is it sad?
Is it inside all you people?
Is it just plain evil?

You've got a lot to learn
You've got a lot to change
You've got nothing to lose
But a ball and chain

Hold my fate, don't make it go away
Grab hold of my fate, we'll make it through the day

Is it good, is it bad?
Is it bitter, is it sad?
Do you really think I need it?
Is it just plain evil?

"SECRET NO MORE"

In a small town everyone knows everyone else's business. It's tiresome and irritating. People telling secrets and making gossip is something I can't get my head around. So I suppose "Secret No More" is a protest song.

Well, well, now what the hell has gotten into you?
Is it something we can make it through?
I spent the best of my life trying to figure you out
Like a black silhouette in a shadow of doubt
Some kind of spectacle that no one can see through

But it burns inside, you hide it well
You hide it from yourself, and you promise that you won't tell
Promise that you won't tell

Secret no more

Now I know that something's wrong
And I'll find out before too long
Only you can break my solitude
Don't you tell anyone I told you this
Gossip can be a deadly kiss
And you got desires to spread your disease too

But it burns inside, you hide it well
You hide in your illusions, and you promise that you won't tell
Promise that you won't tell
Promise that you won't yell

Secret no more

Promise that you won't tell
Promise that you won't yell for help

Secret no more
Secret no more
But I'm keepin' it

"ARTIFICIAL HEART"

I developed a taste for really bad B horror films, which coincided with me becoming obsessed with the idea of how fucked up it is that women are not able to walk alone at night. It's creeped me out my whole life, so I wrote a creepy song about it. Decapitation has always been sort of a fascination for me, too. People lose their heads a lot in my songs. I like that "Artificial Heart" tells a story, and the suggestion is that the woman's fake heart makes her immortal.

It's a secondhand story no one wants to hear
And it's wet with blood, salted with tears
It's black and white and red all over
It happens all the time

This was something about an artificial heart

She lived in a sleepy town trailer-home park
Where not many people go out after dark
Innocent, helpless, and seventeen
Queen of every loser's wet dream

Which brings us to our villain, but a mother could love
He liked amputation and the Lord above
He kidnapped her on her way home from school
She lost her mind, and he lost his cool

She didn't tell him about the artificial heart

Announced missing and dead
Then some kid found her head
Then an arm, and a leg, and you know the rest they said
The artificial heart it was still beating

With a needle and thread they sewed on her head
She's alive and well because she was never dead
She doesn't remember the day she didn't die
Or how everybody cried

She read the story in the paper how she was victimized
And you should have seen the look in her eyes
Her assailant was acquitted and as she read
I swear she laughed off her head

They found her feet in the fridge
and her head in the lake her neck
in the woods he took all she could
take but her artificial heart was
still beating and with a needle and
thread they sewed on her head
she's alive and well guess she was
never dead she just doesn't remember
the day she didn't die and how it
made everybody cry she saw the
story in the paper how she was
victimize you should have seene
the look in her eyes and she read
it out loud and as she read she
just laughed right off her head.

Been arrested for attempted suicide but
somehow he messed up every time he tried
this could never happen to me

"P-9"

I rarely get the opportunity to write a song for an occasion, but this was one of them. I was asked to write a song for the P-9ers, the local UFCW branch in Austin, Minnesota. They were on strike, and it was a desperate situation, picketing in the freezing cold. So Grant Hart from Hüsker Dü and I went into the studio, and we each played on the other's song. He cut one of his songs, "2541," and I brought in "P-9." It's about unions and their right to exist. Other Minnesota artists also contributed to the cause, creating a compilation record to raise awareness for the P-9ers.

Somebody's thinking that there might be something wrong
Business is sinking and the crew's been casted off
Nobody's bailing, nobody's sailing, but we're watching here from shore
Nobody's working
We better work this out

If we could see eye to eye, you could see just exactly who is small
But I do my job, and do it well, and go to hell for writing on the wall
There'd be enough to go around if I could just get around you
I am not down, my hands are empty, and they're open
And I need something to do

And it makes me wonder who I'm working for
'Cause I think you know just what I'm looking for
And it makes me wonder who you're working for
How many children are waiting by your door?
Is this just a job that I'm working for?

You gave me nothing, now you're taking it away
I should be walkin' and make it easy to ignore, but I guess I'd better stay
And I forgave you for the things that you've done wrong
Nobody's working
And it's gone on far too long

And it makes me wonder who you're working for
'Cause I think you know just what I'm looking for
And it makes me wonder who I'm working for
How many children are waiting by your door?
Is it just a paycheck I'm fighting for?

"TAKE IT TO THE ROOT"

*This one's a "scream'a." I just made up the lyrics as I was screaming them.
I'm trying to get to the root of the situation, whatever it may be.*

Hey, what you doing comin' around my place?
I hear you cryin', tears run down my face
Do this, do that, it's always push, push, push
But I sure grow tired of beating 'round the bush

Take it to the root
Take it, take it, take it

Whatcha saying, calling out my name?
I ain't got no shame, better find someone else to blame
Talking 'round in circles, better get to the point
I should find someone else to disappoint

Take it to the root
Take it, take it, take it

I can't take it, always in my face
Don't I know you, I've seen you someplace
Back before you know it, back for more abuse
Back to where I started from, home and on the loose

Take it to the root
Take it, take it, take it

Take it to the root one time
Take it to the root two times
Take it to the root three times
Take it to the root four times muthafuckers

Take it to the root

Twin/Tone Records is pleased to announce the release of the new EP from Soul Asylum, <u>Clam Dip and Other Delights</u>. Postponed so as not to conflict with the release of the <u>Hang Time</u> album, <u>Clam Dip and Other Delights</u> was previously available only in England. The American version features two new tracks, both unreleased studio monsters. "Artificial Heart" is the weirdest, and just about the coolest, song Soul Asylum have ever done, while "Take It to the Root" has been re-dubbed by cover boy Karl Mueller as "MC5 Squared". <u>Clam Dip</u> contains three more originals and a cover of The Wad's "Chains", making for a six-song delight. The enclosed Karl Mueller "stand-up" is only a <u>taste</u> of things to come. **AVAILABLE APRIL 10**.

COLLET AVENUE SOUTH · MINNEAPOLIS MINNESOTA 55404 · 612-872-0646 TELEX: 650-288-1571 FAX: 612-872-9326

HANG TIME

S o, there we were, four bandmates and a soundman, driving around the
country. And then Hollywood or New York comes knockin', and the
paradigm changes. It turns into something more professional. It's punk rock,
though. It's not supposed to be professional, ya know? It's supposed to be
freewheelin', fuckin', art-poetry shit. It's a shitshow; it's a mess. That's what's
beautiful about it. It's chaos. And trying to make chaos professional is a challenge, to say the least.

Luckily for us, the jump to a major label didn't change the band as much
as it changed the way other people felt about the band. People were interested in us, and people apparently saw money in it. So now we're having din-
ner at fancy restaurants and eating food that we have literally never tasted
before. We're all living together in an apartment in the big city, in Manhattan, and money is no object for the first time in my life. So, does this change
the pressure on me as a writer? Absolutely not. Not for me. I didn't give a
fuck. I was just doing what I was doing. And as a band, we maintained our
cynical sense of humor, and our ability to think that, maybe, this was all just
a big joke.

The question was, who would produce the next record? I suggested the
guy who produces the Ramones records, Ed Stasium, and the guy who plays
in Patti Smith's band, Lenny Kaye. It was jaw-dropping to me that they just
said, "Okay." So, a relationship with Lenny Kaye began, and it is alive and
fresh today. He is one of my favorite people. Ed Stasium is just brilliant.

Lenny and Ed started coming to the shows and watching the band,
and they had no intention of changing what we were doing. It was almost
like they were trying to document a freak show from Minneapolis. So, the
record—well, I wrote the fuck out of that record.

"DOWN ON UP TO ME"

"Down on Up to Me" is very literal to what I was feeling in my life at that time. It's up to me to either completely fuck this up or make something out of it, you know?

Dear stranger to authority
Welcome to the minority
It's not someplace you have to go
It's not something you have to know

Don't do this, don't touch that
Draw the line, burn the shrine, speak my mind
Maybe I'll wait for another time

Sometimes good comes to those who wait
Sometimes it makes you hesitate
Some folks fight for humanity
Some folks fight for their sanity

Don't do this, don't do that
Don't try this, don't touch that
Fooled for the last time
By the weight of the world coming down

Down on, down on up to me
Down on up to me
Wait for another time

When you look down on me, I get so uppity
Starting my own army, just me and my friends
You better get friendly

Coming down, down on
Down on up to me
Coming down, down on, down on up to me
Down on up to

Though it might just come down to trust
It sometimes just comes down to lust
That's just one person's point of view

"LITTLE TOO CLEAN"

Oh, here's a bunch of dirty, dirty, punk rock fellas. Now we're figuring out that we can't just be slobs. So, are we part of this earth? Or are we going to get uptight about how shiny our shoes are?

Thought I heard you screaming and pulling out your hair
Furiously steaming, a state upon your stare

Don't you know
Dirt will find you
And dirt reminds you
That dirt will always be there

It's only dirt around you
And dirt surrounds you
It follows you everywhere

Here's a dirty joke, man, filled with filth and smut
The harder that it sparkles, the more it can corrupt

Don't you know
Dirt can't hurt you
I'm truly certain
It usually washes out

Don't you know?
Rain will wash out the stain
And all of your pain
Will work itself out

Work it out

Afraid you've lost your innocence to some odd social scene
You're right on time, but you've been replaced by a shiny new machine

And dirt keeps following you
And you don't know what it means
You're a little too clean

One day dirt will bury you and you will understand
There is nothing much more than the ground on which you stand

Don't you know?
Dirt will find you
And dirt reminds you
That dirt will always be there

It's only dirt around you
And dirt surrounds you
It follows you everywhere

Afraid you've lost your innocence to some odd social scene
You're right on time, but you've been replaced by a shiny new machine

And dirt keeps following you
And you don't know what it means
You're a little too clean

Do The BIZ

Comiming into focus
down to the last crumb
in every grain of sand
bite of a half baked plan
out of my hands

Distraction,
workin without a plan before

I have seen this war before
and woke up on this floor before
its tradition, heroic lore familiar
behind every door of doo wop and
dogma of ashes and sawdust and
all the trust turned into lust but its not us
it happened without a plan
and its getting out of hand
but I'm doin the best I can
doin what we can

Hand me down my shopping cart
I'll buy some art I'll buy some darts
and throw em at my freinds for kicks
and bore them with my dirty trick
Im bettin what I can bet
forget what I can forget
I aint seen nothing yet
and Im taken what I can get

If someday comes early
you'll know where its gone
to take what your learning
and takes you go for all you have learned
The bridges are burned

"SOMETIME TO RETURN"

At this point I'm off; I've left home, I've left Minneapolis. I don't know if I'm ever coming back. My destination is maybe to come back someday. And here I am, more than thirty years later, living in Minneapolis again.

I ran my way
I walked a fine line
Wasted time only to find
That you were calling our thing mine
And to remind me I am fine

What you are is what you see
And you see me, and we can be
Something you can call "we"
We are

Doing what we can
Working without a plan
I'm beginning to understand
It's getting out of hand

I have seen these closing doors
I've woke up on this floor before
Picked it apart for hours, and hours
Hours and hours of turning and tossing
And looking and listening to you
And all the fucked-up things you do

But you're doing the best you can
With every grain of sand
It's trickling through your hand
Sayin' catch me if you can

If someday comes early
Comes whipping, comes whirling
To take you for all you have learned
The tables are turning
The bridges are burning
My destination's sometime to return

Throw away your calendar
And saddle up your salamander
Get up and get down
Ride into town, and look around

Get up and do something
Your time to choose it
Do it

Doing the best I can
With or without a plan
I'm taking what I can get
I haven't seen nothing yet

If one day you wake up
And find what you make up
Come and get me
Come and take me there

Into your illusion
I make my intrusion
Anytime, anyplace, anywhere

The hourglass is draining fast
It knows no future, holds no past
And all this too will come to pass
Never, forever, whatever

If someday comes early
Comes whipping, comes whirling
To take you for all you have learned

The tables are turning
The bridges are burning
My destination's sometime to return

I ran my way I walked a fine line
wasted time only to find that you calling our thing mine
and to remind me I am fine.
and what you are is what you see and
you see me and we can be something we can call we
WORKIN WITHOUT A PLAN DOIN WHAT WE CAN
BEGGINNING TO UNDERSTAND ITS GETTING OUT OF HAND
i swam for dissapearing shores
I've woke up on this floor before.
Traditionell heroic lore familiar behind every door
of doo wop and dogma and ashes + sadclust
and all the trust turned into lust but its not us

IF SOMEDAY COMES EARLY, COMES WHIPPING+WHIRLING
AND TAKES YOU FOR ALL YOU HAVE LEARND
YOUR BRIDGES ARE BURNING THE TABLES ARE TURNING
MY DESTINATIONS' SOMETIME TO RETURN

Throw away your calender and saddle up
your salamander get out get up and get down
ride into town and look around just
get up and do something high time to manage samett
do it do it the best you can the power
is in your hands with or without a plan
in every grain of sand

"BEGGARS AND CHOOSERS"

The difference between rich people and poor people had become painfully obvious to me at this point in my life. "Beggars and Choosers" is a reflection on that idea.

Right before the aftermath, I saw where it would end
They said it was an accident, I guess that all depends
On who you talk to, and who you know
And where you come from, and where you go

In your crowd of pushers and users
Takers and losers
Beggars and choosers

Your childhood days are over, as you stuff your shirt and say
"Made a choice, and wrong or right, it's this way I will stay"
You'll sell it to your children; you'll sell it to your wife
Buying is your business, and selling, it's your life

It's your life
In your crowd of pushers and users
Takers and losers
Beggars and choosers

The vultures are all circling around your withered brow
The scavengers, evangelists will get to you somehow
Your mother and your ex–best friend; the letters that you never send
Your illegitimate children are coming for you now

They're always tracking you down
It's looking like a showdown
Between revenge and the ends you can't defend

Can you try to imagine a story that has no end?
I think you'd better steal it while you still understand it
And sell it to one of your friends

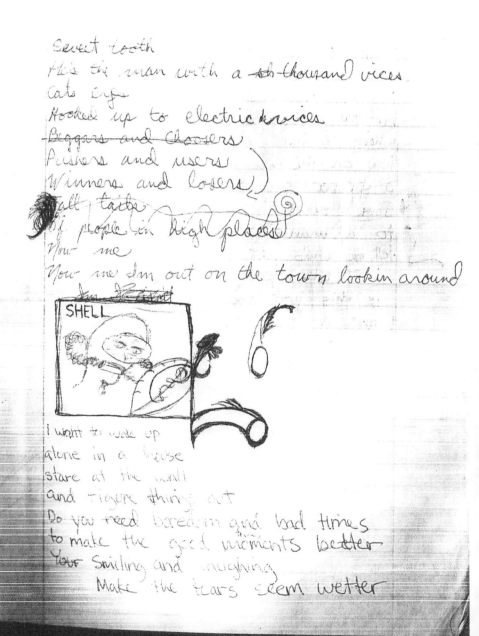

"ENDLESS FAREWELL"

Recently, someone was telling me about the "Minnesota goodbye." I didn't
know that was a thing. As I understand it, the "Minnesota goodbye" is where
you stand in the entryway ready to go, and it takes you forever to actually say
goodbye and leave. Sometimes it's because it's so cold and you don't want to
go outside, and sometimes it's because you're still having a good time hanging
out. Or perhaps it's a little of both.

Anyway, the people I was missing when all these things were going on—
being in New York recording and being away from home all the time—
I always hoped I would see them again someday. Thankfully, most of them
I still know.

Rise and shine, get your razor sharp
Size up yourself in the mirror
A slice of life to last throughout the years

Sooner or later
It all comes back to you
And we will remember
The fine things you can do

I'm giving back all the things that you gave to me
I'm saving up the price to pay to be free
Remember the first time you saw the rising sun
You may be done, but I have just begun

The leaves are burning, and the ashes have blown away
I'm turning over new leaves almost every day

You let 'em think you'd just as soon stay
You let 'em think you had nothing to say
Now you want 'em to just let you go away
To find some fangled security

Some strangled form of purity
To restore your faith in all the things you've come to hate

You give and you take
And you leave it alone
What I want so badly is for this to be a place you can call home

And I haven't felt this way
Since yesterday, or I don't remember when
What I want so badly
To be someone you can call a friend

'Til we meet again
Endless farewell
Hello, again

"STANDING IN THE DOORWAY"

"Standing in the Doorway" is about the choice of whether to cross the threshold and go out into the world or just say "fuck it" and watch TV on the couch. It's probably one of the greatest yin and yang dichotomies in life. That's never going to change.

Standing in the doorway
Wondering if it's safe to go outside
Wondering if I'll come back
Wondering if I might just drift out with the rising tide

Sitting and waiting and hoping to find
Something you're good at to use up your time
To crawl from the ocean and lie on the shore
A moonbeam that rests on the dust on your floor

I'm not going out there
Don't try to tell me I'm paranoid
Wouldn't say I'm not scared
Though it may be safe to say that I am annoyed
In the intersection traffic lights are red in all directions
Everyone breaks the law sometimes
We all break down our foolish pride, and beg for some affection

I can't say I know how you feel
Everyone seems to know how you should
I would if I could help you remember
What it's like to feel good

Chitter and chatter and everything matters
I ask how you're feeling
And you just say, "shattered"
Asleep on the couch with your eyes open wide

Standing in the doorway
Waiting as you come and as you leave
You say get out of my way
Won't you stop and talk about the hectic life you lead

They're all going somewhere
They all have someplace they have to be
Maybe I should join them
I wish I could, I think I have to stay here with me

It brings a tear to your eye to get out into the open
I can't believe I see myself
Coming into focus

Standing in the Door way

Standing in the door way
wonderin' if its safe to go outside
wonderin' if ill come back
wonderin' if I might just float out with the creeping tide

Sitting and waiting and hoping to find
something your good at to use up your time
to crawl from the ocean and lie on the shore
a moonbeam that rests on the dust on your floor

I'm not going out there
don't try to tell me I'm paranoid
wouldn't say I'm not scared
Though it might be safe to still say
that I am anoid
In the intersection traffic lights are red in all direction
Every one breaks the law sometimes everyone
breaks down their pride and begs for some affection

I can't say I know how you feel every one seems
to know how you should I would if i could
just remember what its like to feel good to see it
comin into focus

Chitter and chatter and everything matters
I asked how your felt and you just said "ouch"
I layed over and went back asleep on the couch

Standing in the door way waiting as you come + as you leave

"MARIONETTE"

During my sophomore year of high school, I was dating a girl who later became a women's studies major. She was very active in the women's movement, and she was inspirational as far as turning me onto great women writers. Anyway, the notion that this human being is a puppet, and this puppet is a woman, and she's trying to cut these strings that are basically oppression—I'm pretty sure that's what the song "Marionette" is about.

Marionette, I haven't met you yet
I hear you're good; I hear you're made out of wood
Not quite as blind as you might think she'd be
Her roots run deep; they run as deep as a tree

And they cut off your wings and replaced them with strings
Now the strings attached to everything
It's twisted and tangled and troubled with anger
But somehow you still swing

Tried all my tricks; I tried to steal a kiss
Splinters and slivers stuck all over my lips
She thinks she must be doing something wrong
They're pulling strings, and then they string you along

And they cut off your wings and replaced them with strings
Now the strings attached to everything
It's twisted and tangled, but I got an angle
On just what makes her swing
She's hanging by a string

Stopping at nothing
It's wearing thin

She's off to work; it sometimes spoils her day
You know the boss, he makes her do things his way

Why do you think she's so scared of ya?
What do you think makes her that way?
When push comes to shove, she'll push and shove ya

It doesn't always have to be this way
She's savin' up for a vacation someday

Why do you think she's so scared of ya?
What do you think makes her that way?
When push comes to shove, she'll push and shove ya
It's very hard work when you don't get paid

And they cut off your wings and replaced them with strings

Marienette I haven't met had you yet
I hear your quite good I hear your made out of wood
She's not as blind as you might think she'd be
Her roots run deep, they run as deep as a tree
And i they cut off her wings + replaced them w/ strings
Now theirs strings attached, too every thing
Its twisted + tangled + brewin' frowned with anger
But somehow she you still swings
Tried all my tricks I tried to steal a kiss slivers + splinters stuck
Looking for some one to manipulate
She figures she must have done something wrong strong
She's pullin strings and now she's making you wait
Their pullin her strings and then just string her along
It doesnt always have to be this way
She's savin up for a vacation some day
Chorus: twisted + tangled, but I got an angle
on just what makes her swing
Punchin Judy punchin holes in walls
Punchin in late whos foolin who soon you'll be taking a fall
Why do you think she's so scared of you
What do you think makes her that way
When push comes to shove she'll push + shove you
Its very hard work when you dont get paid

"ODE"

"Ode" is a celebration of street people. Some of the greatest wisdom I have learned has come from talking to strangers and homeless people. People who are on the street. And that's what this song is—an ode to the people who taught me that wisdom.

The idea of being a "casualty" is a theme in the song, too, and that word is fascinating to me. How can a word describe something that is casual and also refer to somebody who dies in a war? There is nothing casual about that.

Well, my friend Jud, he was a fuddy-dud
Chewed his cud, he was a stick in the mud
I swear he hated everyone

And he's bumming nickels and bumming dimes
But most of all, you know, he's just bumming time

And every day was a bad day
They walked out and on and over him
He was turning gray

Never knew love, he gave up on hope
Stayed in bed and stopped using soap
He was a dirty old man

But he never said, "poor little old me"

Well, one fine day he won the lottery
Instant millionaire, without a care
It didn't change a thing

Drove out to Reno
He lost everything at a roadside casino
You know he never made it into town
Where the bright lights trickled down
He was a casualty

He stewed and brewed and he ran out of food
And all he got was more lewd and crude
He was very rude

The only thing he hated worse than the city
Was charity and self-pity
He'd been around
I talked to him, that's what I found
He was a casualty

Poor little ol' me
Poor, poor casualty

"JACK OF ALL TRADES"

It would seem that I'm talking about myself a lot on this record. "Jack of All Trades" is me wondering how my life is going to turn out, and acknowledging that being good at a lot of things is maybe better than thinking you're the best at one thing.

If I could be anything I wanted, I don't know
I'd be stuck here with myself, being average Joe
But if I could be like a jack-of-all-trades, yes, I'd have it made

Glass blower, flamethrower, grass mower, firefighter
I'm trying to loosen up, or make it tighter

The jack-of-all-trades
Master of nothing
Let's try it again
The jack-of-all-trades
Sometimes he gets paid
Wait for your lucky day

See my train; now it's gone
Brings it down to the bone
You stutter and you stall
When you hear the piper call
Dream tracing and rat racing
Late timing, outta placin', down the hall
The piper calls

I'll try anything, sometimes I just can't say no
I'm learnin' to dig with my hands
I'm learnin' to work with my mind
So much to lose, and so much left to find
So much to take, so much to leave behind

I walked down this fucking street
You never know who you might meet
See the signs up ahead
Tellin' me you're half dead
Say your prayers; put you to bed

At the end of the day stands the jack-of-all-trades
And the fool he has made
It's a jack-of-all-trades, and the fool he has made
Of himself and his friends

But he'd do it again, yes, he'd do it again
He's the jack

If I could be anything I want, but then I don't know
I'd be stuck bein my self anyway its all I know
But if I could be like a Jack of all Trades
Yes I'd have it made, bein Jack of all Trade
It would be all right to live a life of a fine writer
glass blower flame thrower vegitabal grower
brave fire fighter (or just about anything)
Oh the jack of all trades
Master of Nothin'
He'll try anything Na Na Na Na Na
Can't do nothing special
Im the jack of all trades
sometimes I get paid Na Na Na Na Na
halls of insuficiancy echos. through your dignity
you stutter and you stall when when you here the
II try anything Save time I just can't say no
Iever know might turn me on last too qiuta go
on know me I cant tern down
In prepare to pay the

"TWIDDLY DEE"

My fascination with language can be over the top, especially when it comes to music, and that comes out in "Twiddly Dee." There are nonsense words, but they come from somewhere in my past. Like, "hey gabba, hi gabba" is from the Ramones. "Twiddly-dee, fe-fo-fi-fum" comes from nursery rhymes. All that shit. It's very, very fast folk music.

Twiddly-dee, fe-fo-fi-fum
There's a giant sleeping, and his pants are undone
He shows no pity for anyone
He's sure to be killed before the morning comes

Twiddle my fingers, and I twiddle my thumbs
Ain't gonna quit 'til my work is all done
I'm a high-society skid row bum
Well on my way to kingdom come

Well, I twiddle in the middle of the moon and sun
I'm wishing and dreaming I'm a special someone
Ain't laying my load on anyone
It's way too high, and it weighs a ton

Do-re-mi, fe-fo-fi-fum
I'm a slave to my music, it's my father and son
I'd never force it on anyone
Can't keep it a secret, so I keep it on the run

They may say what they say, about the way that we stay
They may do what they do, about the things that we do

Hey diddle-diddle, seen you spittle your rum
I ain't worried about the dumb things I've done
Ain't worried about the dumb things to come
When I smell the blood of a little bit of fun

Hey diddy, hi diddy, ho-hi-hum
Sometimes I wanna be friends with everyone
My friends tell me it can't be done
Then some days I feel I don't know anyone

Now what goes up doesn't always come down
You'll never believe the things I've found
Amazing what you learn just hanging around
Can't put a square peg in a hole that's round

They may say what they say, about the way that we stay
They may do what they do, about the things that we do

Hey gabba, hi gabba, doo-da-day
Ain't for winning or for losing it's the pleasure to play
Work all night and I sleep all day
Yes, I guess I'm lucky, I can live my own way

"HEAVY ROTATION"

"Heavy Rotation" is a good ender for the record. I was very close to calling this song "I am, I am, I am, I am, I am, I am, I am, I am." It's an odyssey of the identity, which somehow resolves itself in being "the human sponge"—as in, I'm just trying to deal with the way I am, and I'm trying to absorb everything.

Order in this court you call my own
Confusion is the order I am shown

Some things don't come easy
Something's got to give
You just might have to waste your life just to live

Now did you think that I was somebody?
And did you think this was somewhere?
I will still be there
So, watch out

Well, I got the right to free myself of fear
Stand over me and watch me disappear
A senseless defense to build another fence
To keep them out, to keep them in
I don't know enemies, just differences

I am the one that soaks it up
I am the one that takes a plunge
And I am the human sponge

Could I be so serious, or am I just too curious
Or just afraid to look away
For missing something you might say

'Cause you've got so much I can borrow
One more debt I can't repay
Tomorrow brings just one more chance to throw it all away
I'm just trying to live with today
And I'm just trying to live with the way
The way I am

Collect all your sense and build another fence
too keep them out too keep them in I don't know
enemys just differenses.
could it be so seriouse or am I just
too curiouse. afraid too give myself away
listen too what you might say

Tomorrow brings just one more chane
to throw it all away

full of lines for you to tap
it in for a thinking kap
don't touch that
touch this don't do that hey
your life for you ..... tell you what to do
always talked about
never figured out
that funny twisted
scared too deathe of mingling
with your advice too me
what this does too me
to the acadamy
get the best of me
everything your read

SOUL ASYLUM AND THE HORSE THEY RODE IN ON

AND THE HORSE THEY RODE IN ON

And the Horse *They Rode in On* was our second major-label record release. We recorded it in California, live on a sound stage with producer Steve Jordan. It was the band's introduction to how great players play. Everything was played live, so we were put on the spot. It was exciting, but it led to a lot of nervous energy, and a lot of outtakes.

I was living in Minneapolis at the time, and it felt like the band was sort of floundering. The "grunge" or "alternative" expressions hadn't really emerged yet. So, we were a punk rock band on a major label, and no one knew what to do with us.

I was trying to grow as a writer and a player, and the album was kind of a giant step for me. *Hang Time* had been so dense, and I felt like opening up a little more, whatever that means. My head was in a strange place. Lyrically, musically, attitude-wise—I was searching and flailing and focusing, all at the same time. The extreme contrast between the song "We 3," which was soft and sweet, and a song like "All the King's Friends," which was hard and brutal, was indicative of the wide range of approaches I was taking with the music on this record. In this way, my writing wasn't really mainstream writing; it was different. There weren't a lot of people doing what we were doing.

Over the years, I have had Soul Asylum enthusiasts say to me that *And the Horse They Rode in On* is their favorite Soul Asylum record. Whether they're aware of it or not, I think they are responding to the live aspect of the recording. There isn't a lot of bullshit, overdubs, and fancy production added in. It was not conceptual; it was just "play it, and play it as good as you can." We weren't relying on Pro Tools; probably because Pro Tools hadn't been invented yet.

"SPINNIN'"

"Spinnin'" is a metaphor about things that make your head spin, while you depend on other people to help you keep your sanity. Still, the world continues to spin, regardless of all your silly foibles.

Follows me wherever we go
Undermining all that we know
Ya suddenly start thinkin'
You've been fooled from the beginnin'
When the cause is lost you find there is no point in winnin'
Then it's hard to think straight, when your head it keeps on spinnin'

If I lost my mind, would you help me find it?

Maybe it's you, maybe it's me
Things aren't quite the way they should be
And now it seems my peace of mind has come up for the biddin'
All those I respect and trust I guess they were just kiddin'
And they will say it's me who's lost, and just sit there grinnin'
My little world has lost control, but still it keeps on spinnin'

If I lost my mind, would you help me find it?
If I lost my mind, I wouldn't have to be reminded

If I lost my mind, I'm not sure I would mind
Would you help me find it?
If I lost my mind, would you help me?

"BITTER PILL"

By this point in my life, I had had to put up with a lot of shit. I realized that swallowing the proverbial bitter pill was what it was going to take for me to get where I needed to go.

It was a brutal experience recording the vocals on "Bitter Pill." Steve Jordan, the producer, locked me in a bathroom with the lights out, and he said, "you're not coming out until you sing this song." It's a very angry vocal performance.

At the end of the track there's a two-bit shack
When you die that's where you go
Down the line there's a bottomless pit
At the end of your rainbow

That's one too many flights of stairs

One more stair and almost there
One more dose of close
One last glare at the bottom of the stairs
One more unholy ghost

Keep coming back to haunt you
Got no place left to go
Meet me on the strip where the strippers all strip
And they'll strip your car to the bone

The queen of the scene tripped on her crown
And the jester started laughing
In a second she said, "remove his head"
I guess that's what you get for laughing

two bit shack when you die thats
where you got
Just down the line theres a pot of   bottomless pit
gold at the end of your rainbow
But thats one to many flights of stair
one more time for almost there
its one more dose of close
its one more glare at the bottom of the
stairs its one   re unholy ghost
kee   to haunt now
to go
your ice cube tra
2 of snow   melting off
orner theirs
almost their
close
the bottom of the sta
ghost
rying now the
e the groom took
alice full of pois
pretty quick
e he fell from g
at almost their
st their
ost
eirs are evil forc
noes
hest and all y
our toes
ke a foul disguarded

At the end of the track theirs a two bit shack
when you die thats where you go
Just down the line theirr a bottomless pit
at the end of your rainbow
But thats one to many fights of stairs
and one last stare at almost their
one more dose of close
one last glare at the bottom of the stairs
one more unholey ghost
keep comin back to haunt you got no place else to go
meet me on the strip where the strippers strip the strip
well the queen of the scene she stripped on her roab
and jesters just started laughing
in a second she said please remove bothe
their heads I guess thats what you get for laughin
and thats on last laugh that lived to tell
just one more pompouse circumstance
one more fool to follow
just another finger down my throat
one bitter pill to swollow
well I see my train a comin
and its moving much to slow
just who it is thats asleep at the wheel
I dont want to know, They took the world for gran
they took the world by storm most of em either
ended up dead or wishin' the had never been born
Just around the the corner theirs
Somebody their to take you their
Dont worry child your sure to be scared

one more drink before I go
one last good luck kiss
one less thing to call my own
One more thing I miss

One less laugh that lived to tell
One more pompous circumstance
One more fool to follow
Another finger down my throat
It's a bitter pill to swallow

I see my train coming
It's moving much too slow
Who is it asleep at the wheel?
I don't want to know

Just around the corner there's
Somebody there to take you there
Don't worry child, you're sure to be scared

One more drink before I go
One last good-luck kiss
One less thing to call my own
That's one more thing I miss

Took the world for granted
Took the world by storm
Most of 'em either ended up dead
Or wishing they had never been born

And just around the corner there's
One more pompous circumstance
One more fool to follow
Another finger down my throat
It's a bitter pill to swallow

"VEIL OF TEARS"

I think I got the expression "veil of tears" from the book Pop. 1280 *by Jim Thompson. You learn to walk a balancing act, and it's all about yin and yang, darkness and light, and overcoming obstacles and getting on with it.*

Well, a fascinating sensation
You know I can't even feel it
I just had to let you know
I can't conceal it

I was recently considering
Taking the pain with the pleasure
Just to find my way to the bottom of this
I'll have to dig forever
And it's no small measure

Lift up your veil of tears

Don't be disappointed, child
If your prayers go unanswered
We are not responsible
For these sad circumstances

Secret agents and freedom fighters
On those impossible missions
Better put your toys and games away
Maybe take the kids out fishing for a buried treasure

Lost in your early years
Behind your veil of tears

So frustrated
Get up anyway
So complicated
Changes every day

'Til the darkness fades
And the light
Will come shining through

I heard the eyes that look to a better world
Always hide beneath a veil of tears

And you hide no more
Lift up your veil of tears
Hide no more
Behind your veil of tears

Now the executioner
Must be executed
I think we'll set him free instead
Watch him run

And you hide no more
Lift up your veil of tears
Hide no more

"NICE GUYS (DON'T GET PAID)"

Story songs are some of my favorite songs. "Nice Guys (Don't Get Paid)"
goes into a fairy tale of sorts, where it's cowboys and drug dealers, and bad
people with good intentions, and good people with bad intentions.

As a band, we'd always embrace the "kill 'em with kindness" motto, as
opposed to turning into real fucking pricks. Then you gradually realize that
maybe the reason you're not making any money is that you're not being
mean, greedy, volatile people. This song spins a yarn about how people with
bad intent are often the ones who are running things. And good little sweet-
hearts just get left in the dust with no money and big problems.

Well, they packed up their violin cases of the finest artillery
Hopped in a big, black Studebaker; they were acting pretty scary
And no one talked as they synchronized their watches
And drove past the train station

Well, the train rolled out with a passenger car
Filled with retired millionaires and movie stars
Two twitching men clutching six-guns in their sweat-drenched coats
With a fail-safe holdup plan, and that would be all she wrote

And the gangsters, cowboys, gypsies, and freewheelers
Sold out their trades to become drug dealers
There ain't no money in doing things straight
Your community thanks you; business is good
And nice guys don't get paid

Outside the train window fast as he could ride
Was a kid on a horse, with a head full of lies
And the tears of excitement couldn't put out the fire in his eyes
For the house, he was riding to burglarize

All through the house they were dancing and singing
An extended family of fiddlers and magicians
A juggler and a chemist who'd invent a potion
To pacify all the killers and rapists

The chemist died in the burglary, and they sold the prescription
For a case of cheap red wine to a traveling salesman
In a three-wheeled jalopy he bought and sold potions
To the city that looked over the ocean

And he sold the last drop, it was big with the rich kids
And soon the city would be crawling with addicts
In back rooms, dark alleys, basements, and attics
Where a fly is trapped in a spider's web, but the bat's got the spider

And no one knows what's going on
But you gotta show up for yourself at the end of the day
And nice guys don't get paid
Nice guys don't get paid

Now all the hopeless romantics are wearing white collars
Upstanding assassins, clean hands, filthy dollars
Hijackin' fanatics who kill for religion
In a city full of addicts, and colored television

"SOMETHING OUT OF NOTHING"

Music is like a spirit. It's conjured; you don't even start with a piece of clay.
You start with an idea. You start with something that is nothing. It still feels
like I'm making something out of nothing, like I don't have a tangible skill.
But if you love something enough, you can make something out of it.

Well if there's one thing that I know
It's easy to kill what's hard to grow
One thing I might say
No one got nowhere by running away

Trying to make something out of nothing
Leaning hard on yet another crutch
All of these temptations keep me wanting
To feel your touch

It's not supposed to make you feel so helpless
Selfless
Crying for some tenderness
I miss your kiss
Impossible to resist

Find somebody to support my habit
Suffering an underdose of love
All of these temptations keep me wanting
The sky above

Oh, my desperate disposition
Keeps me bitching
Keeps me wishing
Wishing for some shelter from within

There ain't nothing I can't live with
Nothing I can't live without

I want this, I want that
I'm wanting just a little slack
It's like an itch that I can't scratch
I got to get this monkey off my back

Trying to make something out of nothing
I can't live without

Wanting nothing

Oh, my desperate disposition
Keeps me bitching
Keeps me wishing
Wishing for some shelter from within

It's not supposed to make you feel this way

One way ticket

If there's one thing I know
It's easy to kill what it's hard to grow
If there's one thing I might say
No one gone no where by runnin away
I'm Trying to make something out of nothing
making not enough seem like to much *(tryin to carry a shot gun fro a touch)*
Ihrying to get a handle on the real thing
trying to keep from falling out of tought tough
its not enough to make me go away
its not enough to make me want to stay
taint nothing I cant live without
There's a new face in my place
Seems my race has run its race
well that's so sad it to bad
now I can't think cause I just get mad
trying to make something out of nothing
Trying to get religion out of pain
trying to find something to believe it
anything just to keep myself sane *(why couldn't I have been ple)*
with work and faith anything possible if you stay with ple

"BRAND NEW SHINE"

There's nothing new under the sun. What's new is old, and what was once old is new again; things tend to go away and come back. That's a big part of music. Something that sounds new to you might sound archaic to someone else. It just got a new shine.

I daresay, this is probably true in all walks of life. There's always some trendy, new, shitty thing that isn't actually new. Perhaps I should just stick to the Levi's and the Converse.

I've got something special to show you
But I suppose you've seen it all before
There's one thing I'm trying to tell you
But then again you've heard it all before

I survived another week, just like the one before
When everything you wanted, somehow leaves you wanting more
And I looked beneath the carpet, behind each and every door
Trying to find you something like you've never had before

And it seems we're just beginners
No previous experience at all
Just the last original sinners
And if you need me just be sure to call

And they tell you which way not to go, and so you go that way
One child plays with what another throws away
Like a kite without string, go anywhere, do anything
I'm trying to take you someplace you've never been before

I see something new in each and every move
From your old, old hat to your blown-out shoes
It's tried and true, and it's all I do
And I hope it's not all the same to you

The old and new, they get mistaken all the time
Is that something I've never seen before?
Or just a brand new shine?

Now they're cranking 'em out by the millions
They look and act exactly just the same
And each one's one in a million
And each has got its own elusive game

It's the same old dusty atmosphere, like the other place
I see something familiar, in each and every face
Seems to me I've seen you, been here, said this once before
I'm trying to take you someplace you've never been before

I see something new in each and every move
From your old, old hat to your blown-out shoes
When I dropped it and broke it, I thought of you
And I hope it's not all the same to you
And the old and new, they get mistaken all the time
Is there something I've never seen before?
Or just a brand new shine?

"EASY STREET"

The first verse of this song could be a premonition. I guess things were so melodramatic that I began to worry about, what if I needed to talk to a friend, and my friend didn't pick up the phone? Then I turned that around to ask, what if my friend was in need, and I didn't pick up the phone? And then I turned that into a friend of a friend. Anyway, whoever it is, the person answers after all.

"Easy Street" concludes with the notion, "if we ever get there, let me know, but I've enjoyed the ride." I was always wondering if the band would ever get to a point where we could pay our friends and pay the rent and not have to worry about everything. I'm not getting my hopes up.

Did you hear the one about the friend of a friend who tried to end it all?
At the last moment he picked up the phone and gave you a call
You thought about letting it ring
But you answered after all
And there you were, put on the spot, at the end of the other line

For all the questions that you never thought you'd ever have to answer to
Who do you turn to when the ones you always turn to go and turn on you?
It leaves you in the dark
Feeling for a switch to turn it on again
You turn it on again

There are no easy answers
The questions remain tough
There's no shortcuts to Easy Street
No corners you can cut
Can you cut this diamond in the rough?

And it's good to see you alive
Sign, your will to survive
Look into your heart before it sees its final hour
Live today like there is no tomorrow

Beyond this mess ahead there is a street
So very hard to find
Though I have thought to lay my head down at this dead end so many times
If we ever get to Easy Street
You can say with a smile
"I came just for the ride"

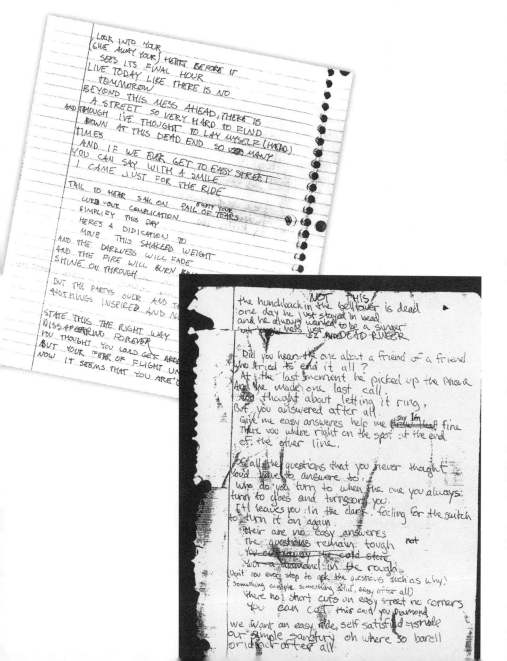

"GROUNDED"

I've always been into symbolism and shapes and numbers. I thought "when eight turns sideways" was a clever way to start a song—as if an eight-year-old just realized the immensity of infinity. For some reason, this concept turns into being on a plane and getting your wings and realizing that you can go anywhere.

Of course, the expression "you gotta stay grounded" can have multiple meanings. Most people say it when they're telling you that you need to keep it together. But staying grounded can also refer to when your plane is delayed and you're on the tarmac, not knowing if you're going to be sitting there for five minutes or five hours, but you hope to be up in the air eventually.

When eight turns sideways
You head on down the highway
Say this is my way
Disappearing forever

But there ain't just one way
So you choose the fun way
Slide on down the runway
On a ticket that goes two ways

And by the way that it sounded
You thought that you'd be astounded
But you left it like you found it
'Cause it wasn't yours to take

What once seemed like dying
Soon turned into flying
So you settle for trying
And you wish you were grounded

No, you cannot get much higher
Than your utmost desire
So you bring it down to size and
Now it seems that you are grounded

By the way that it sounded
You thought that you'd be astounded
But you left it like you found it
Now you find that you are grounded

"BE ON YOUR WAY"

"Be on Your Way" is an adventure song. It's taking you on a ride. It's about perpetual motion: living and learning and growing up and trying to be cool. I don't mean "cool" in a Fonzie sort of way, but more keeping your shit together and not letting alienation hold you back.

Just like an old man in the candy store
The riots across the street
The cold greets the newborn
The neighbors that never meet

No one's making plans here
No one knows for sure
The way to keep it inside
It's just one more door opening for you
And whatever you do
When everything still seems new
It's sure to come to something to change the rest of your life

For a chance to feel normal
But now you're in too deep
Pace like the circles around your eyes
The rest of the world's fast asleep

No sense of direction
No sense at all
No one there to break your fall
No one knows what's happening to you
I never quite got that through
No one waits for you
And no one calls with something to do with the rest of your life

Stop looking over my shoulder
Little wiser, a little bolder
If you're going somewhere
I might be on your way

This time I don't mean maybe
Nowhere I'd rather be
If you're coming with me I might be on your way

I saw you there on the corner
With my name written all over you
I was trying to get your attention
It's all I ever wanted from you

Who will be the victim?
Who will be the host?
Who will you take it out on for not being there?
When you needed them most for you
I'm coming to terms with you
And you can pull me through
I'm settling up with something to change the rest of my life
Something to do with the rest of my life
I need something to feel the rest of my life's not in vain

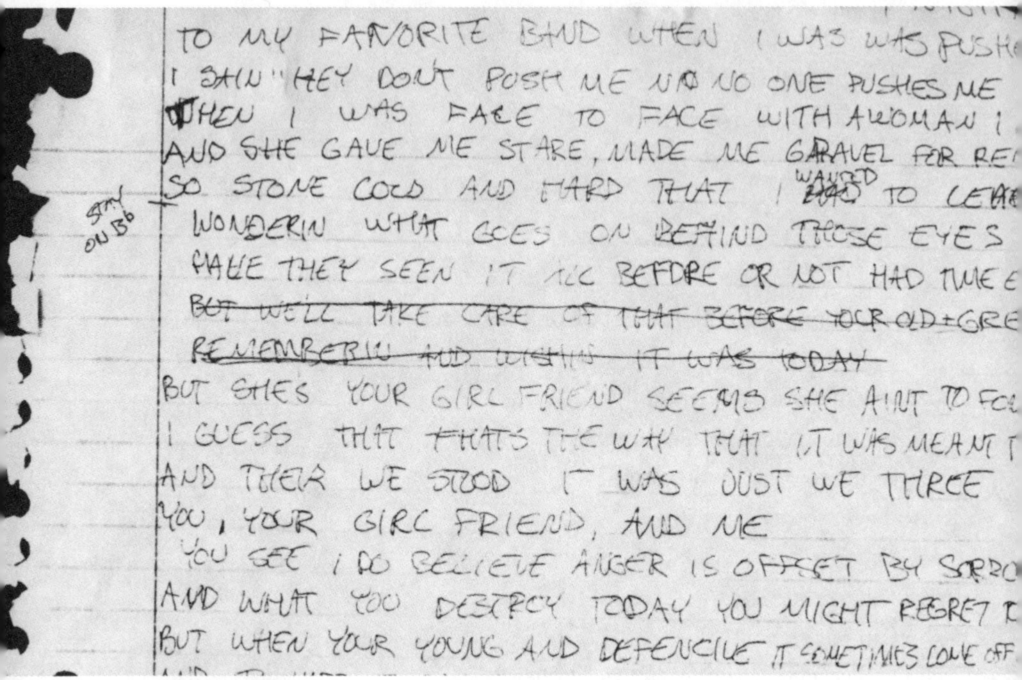

[Handwritten manuscript page:]

TO MY FAVORITE BAND WHEN I WAS WAS PUSH
I SAID "HEY DON'T PUSH ME NO NO ONE PUSHES ME
WHEN I WAS FACE TO FACE WITH A WOMAN I
AND SHE GAVE ME STARE, MADE ME GRAVEL FOR RE
SO STONE COLD AND HARD THAT I WANTED TO LEAVE
WONDERIN WHAT GOES ON BEHIND THOSE EYES
HAVE THEY SEEN IT ALL BEFORE OR NOT HAD TWEE
BUT WELL TAKE CARE OF THAT BEFORE YOUR OLD+GRE
REMEMBERIN AND WISHIN IT WAS TODAY
BUT SHES YOUR GIRL FRIEND SEEMS SHE AINT TO FO
I GUESS THAT THATS THE WAY THAT IT WAS MEANT T
AND THEIR WE STOOD I WAS JUST WE THREE
YOU, YOUR GIRL FRIEND, AND ME
YOU SEE I DO BELIEVE ANGER IS OFFSET BY SORRO
AND WHAT YOU DESTROY TODAY YOU MIGHT REGRET T
BUT WHEN YOUR YOUNG AND DEFENCIVE IT SOMETIMES COME OFF

"WE 3"

The meaning of "We 3" seems pretty apparent in the lyrics. Everybody's had experience being the third wheel, being ignored, no one noticing you standing there. There have been times in my life when I've loved being the third wheel. The idea of being a third wheel can relate to a living situation, or a club situation, or the whole "three is a crowd" thing as well.

I was tapping my foot
On a Friday night
To my favorite band
I was pushed aside

I said, "Hey, don't push me. No one pushes me"
When I was face-to-face with a woman I admired

And she gave me this look I could not believe
And the cold stare remained, and I wanted to leave

See I do believe anger is offset by sorrow
What you destroy today, you might regret tomorrow

When you're young and defensive, it comes off offensive
And it's hard to repay the tolerance that you've borrowed

The lasting relationship sinks right off the pier
Who wears the pants?
It's faded but clear

She's your girlfriend, seems she ain't too fond of me
I guess that that's the way it was meant to be
There we were, just we 3
You, your girlfriend, and me

I've known you forever
You two just met
So easily amused
How fast we forget

It ain't my jealousy or my self-righteous greed
She's a bit like a book I'm too farsighted to read

And I wish you the best
I sometimes feel the need
To say, "remember me"

She's your girlfriend, as far as we can see
Does she look at you the way she looks at me?
And here we are, just we 3
You, your girlfriend, and me

She's your girlfriend, it's getting harder to see
Better just take her home, better just let it be
When she walks out that door
You'll come looking for me

"ALL THE KING'S FRIENDS"

"There's men without gods, and gods without men." I was really happy with myself when I came up with that line. The song "All the King's Friends" is basically about the hierarchy that is church and state, leaders and followers, and kings and subjects. It seems like people need someone to look up to, and that can often lead to abusive relationships. I never put a lot of faith in "leaders." The idea of a leader who's just running things with his cronies, his friends, and his equally jaded counterparts is terrifying. And it couldn't be more relevant than in the Trump era.

The papers read that the king is dead
The people said what we need instead
Is to be on our own

But people they do the strangest things
You never know what they might do
When they are left alone

There's men without gods, and gods without men
And a spirit of which none of them can transcend
But something peculiar is happening
We should just be happy with just what we've got
And the problems should be too few to mention
But they're not

Where can I go for some information?
So tired of the big sensation
I need to know what's going on

Oh well, you're the well informed
Into your world, which I was born
My friend, here's to you

How would I know if there was something wrong
When the weak of heart out-survive the strong
The truth is almost always confidential
You never know just what you've got until it's gone
And your friends have never seemed so essential
When you're wrong

Remarkably incredible, incredibly forgettable
I know this might sound strange, don't ever change
Amazingly un-faceable, entirely replaceable
There's nothing I would rearrange, don't ever change

Out of luck, out of space, out of time, out of place
Don't try to save face, my friend

There was a time and there was a place
For your face and for your race, but it's been swept away

GRAVE DANCERS UNION

The band always joked about a black cloud that followed us around. During this period, if we weren't in the studio, we were on the road, and we weren't really getting anywhere with A&M. I was disillusioned and depressed, and I thought I was going deaf. My brain was doing things I had never experienced before, and not necessarily in a good way. I was introduced to a psychiatrist in a mental ward, and that's when I realized I was really losing it. I was in full retreat. Even though by this time the band had developed a hardened sense of humor and we had embraced the idea of laughing in the face of adversity, this was a really bad time for me.

All this emotional trauma spilled into the writing of the record. It's what makes *Grave Dancers Union* so raw. This was the first time I really started writing with an acoustic guitar, very much by myself. Alone. Before that, we would often work out arrangements in the practice space and jam out on things and decide together how long parts should be and whatnot during practice.

Anyway, we recorded the demo for *Grave Dancers Union* in our practice space, and it was all acoustic. I took the cassette to New York and went to six or seven different record labels, and talked to people, and played the stuff for them. I started noticing a similar response. I think the guy at Geffen Records said, "So, is this a down record?" And I'm like, what does that even mean? I couldn't hear the material the way other people did. And I wasn't attached to the perception of the band that other people had.

Still, people wanted the band. The "rock and roll" band was suddenly sought after again. Bands like us that were out on the road with this DIY aesthetic, we didn't really need much help. We knew what we were doing and had built up our own fan base. We had played all over the world by then.

When Columbia Records signed the band, they gave us the resources to do everything and anything we wanted. So now we had the ability to work with great producers and studios. Michael Beinhorn produced *Grave Dancers Union*. He was a perfectionist, scrutinizing every little, tiny sound— but we had the time to get it right. We worked very hard on this record, because we could.

"SOMEBODY TO SHOVE"

Recently I learned about a little girl who got in trouble with her teacher at school for singing "Somebody to Shove" because the teacher said it promoted violence. Much to my approval, her parents thought that was ridiculous. Both the kid and her parents seemed to understand the song is about motivation.

Grandfather watches the grandfather clock
And the phone hasn't rang for so long
And the time flies by like a vulture in the sky
Suddenly he breaks into song

I'm waiting by the phone
Waiting for you to call me up and tell me I'm not alone

Hello, speak up, is there somebody there?
These hang-ups are getting me down
In a world frozen over with overexposure
Let's talk it over; let's go out and paint the town

'Cause I'm waiting by the phone
Waiting for you to call me up and tell me I'm not alone
'Cause I want somebody to shove
I need somebody to shove
I want somebody to shove me

You're a dream for insomniacs
Prize in the Cracker Jack
All the difference in the world is just a call away

And I'm waiting by the phone
Waiting for you to call me up and tell me I'm not alone

Yes, I'm waiting by the phone
I'm waiting for you to call me
Come call me and tell me I'm not alone
'Cause I want somebody to shove
I need somebody to shove
I want somebody to shove me

"BLACK GOLD"

When I was in fourth grade, I was supposed to pick a book from the library and make a report. I found a book called Black Gold. *I don't remember anything about the book, but the expression stuck.*

I was involved in a protest of President George H. W. Bush's war in Iraq, and people were carrying signs that said, "no blood for oil." It dawned on me that oil—sometimes referred to as "black gold"—is so often the cause for war. It just seems painful and unnecessary.

Two boys on a playground
Tryin' to push each other down
See the crowd gather 'round
Nothing attracts a crowd like a crowd

Black gold in a white plight
Won't you fill up the tank, let's go for a ride
I don't care 'bout no wheelchair
I've got so much left to do with my life

Moving backwards through time
Never learn, never mind
That side's yours, this side's mine
Brother you ain't my kind

You're a black soldier, white fight
Won't you fill up the tank, let's go for a ride
Sure'd like to feel some pride
But this place just makes me sad inside

Mother, do you know where your kids are tonight?

Keeps the kids off the streets
Gives them something to do, something to eat
This spot was a playground
This flat land used to be a town

Black gold in a white plight
Won't you fill up the tank, let's go for a ride
Sure'd like to feel some pride
But this place just makes me feel sad inside

Black gold in a white plight
Won't you fill up the tank, let's go for a ride
I don't care 'bout no wheelchair
I've got so much left to do with my life

"RUNAWAY TRAIN"

I had a melody with some words in my head; I believe it was called "Two Souls." It wouldn't go away. A couple years later I still had it stuck in my head. I sat down and wrote the words, and I didn't think much of it after that. But the song "Runaway Train" is trying to explain a dark time.

Call you up in the middle of the night
Like a firefly without a light
You were there like a blowtorch burning
I was a key that could use a little turning

So tired that I couldn't even sleep
So many secrets I couldn't keep
Promised myself I wouldn't weep
One more promise I couldn't keep

It seems no one can help me now
I'm in too deep
There's no way out
This time I have really led myself astray

Runaway train never going back
Wrong way on a one-way track
Seems like I should be getting somewhere
Somehow I'm neither here nor there

Can you help me remember how to smile?
Make it somehow all seem worthwhile
How on earth did I get so jaded?
Life's mystery seems so faded

I can go where no one else can go
I know what no one else knows
Here I am just drowning in the rain
With a ticket for a runaway train

And everything seems cut and dry
Day and night
Earth and sky
Somehow I just don't believe it

Runaway train never going back
Wrong way on a one-way track
Seems like I should be getting somewhere
Somehow I'm neither here nor there

Bought a ticket for a runaway train
Like a madman laughing at the rain
A little out of touch, a little insane
It's just easier than dealing with the pain

Runaway train never going back
Wrong way on a one-way track
Seems like I should be getting somewhere
Somehow I'm neither here nor there

Runaway train never coming back
Runaway train tearing up the track
Runaway train burning in my veins
Runaway, but it always seems the same

"KEEP IT UP"

I used to be in a side project called Golden Smog. Even though I had stopped playing with them by this point, I was asked to do a song with them at First Avenue. I didn't know what to sing, so I just wrote "Keep It Up." It's meant to be super easy to learn. As far as I remember, they had to play it and just sort of follow me. I honestly don't remember if we rehearsed it. We might have played it at sound check. I just wanted to write a fun, simple song that people could play without really practicing. And I wanted to write a song that had "Na na, na . . ." in it.

I'm down here waitin' on a shattered heart
I'm gonna put it back together if it tears me apart
If I can keep it up

I've been complaining like a broken record
Gonna get what I want if it takes forever
If I can keep it up

Though the rain weighs down your wings
Still the caged bird's got to sing
Singing, "Na na, na . . ."

I know it seems funny tryin' to understand
It's just that things don't always go the way you planned
Still you keep it up

Nothin' in the world's gonna keep me down
I'm just holdin' out, just hangin' around
Tryin' to keep it up
Just to keep it up

Though the rain weighs down your wings
Still the caged bird's got to sing
Singing, "Na na, na . . ."

Keep it up

747's gonna take us away
Take us up to heaven, gonna be okay
If we can keep it up

Though the rain weighs down your wings
Still the caged bird's got to sing
Singing, "Na na, na . . ."

Keep it up

"HOMESICK"

*I remember what the hotel room looked like where I wrote "Homesick"—
which is really strange because most hotel rooms kind of look the same. It was
a cheap one, I know that. The touring had become endless. I don't even think
I was paying rent anywhere. I had given up having a place in Minneapolis.
This song reflects a very distinct feeling I had of not really knowing where
to live and of missing people.*

I want to live with you
In the fifth dimension
In a dream I've never had
'Cause I just can't live like this
In a world like this
I just want a kiss goodbye

We are not of this world
And there's a place for us
Stuck inside this fleeting moment
Tucked away where no one owns it
Wrapped up in a haste
And by mistake got thrown away

I am so homesick
But it ain't that bad
'Cause I'm homesick for the home I've never had

And though I sometimes get annoyed
I know just where I'm at
This is my song of joy
And now I know there are no secret tricks
No correct politics
Just liars and lunatics

We are not of this world
And there's a place for us
Stuck inside this fleeting moment
Tucked away where no one owns it
Wrapped up in a haste
And by mistake got thrown away

I am so homesick
But it ain't that bad
'Cause I'm homesick for the home I've never had

And though I would not take it personally
It's just the child in me
Who never really knew how much I had

Woe is me, I am so homesick
But it ain't that bad
'Cause I'm homesick for the home I've never had

"GET ON OUT"

Around this time, it felt like my brain was maturing in a way that it was embracing all these wonderful things like clinical depression, and anxiety, and other emotions that seemed to be intensifying in a bad way. I suppose I was feeling super insecure about being in a rock band and just wondering how the fuck I was going to continue to do it.

I gotta get on
I gotta get on out
All these worried troubled thoughts gotta get on out of my head
Gotta get on out of my head

Will I be on the streets tomorrow?
Will I have to beg and borrow?
Will I have to go back to the job I left behind?
Could you still make it, with a guy who never made it?
Would you look into my eyes if I were to go blind?

I gotta get on
Gotta get on out
All these worried troubled thoughts gotta get on out of my head
Gotta get on out of my head

Now will you leave me for another?
Send me running back to mother?
Will I have the time to tell you how I really feel?
Am I just getting slower, or are you just talking faster?
Do we need bad disaster to make it plain to see?

That all these worried troubled thoughts gotta get on out of my head
Gotta get on out of my head

Do I just feel like cryin'?
'Cause I'm sick and tried of tryin'
Trying to convince you this ain't how it has to be
The ground you walk on's sacred
The sky above awaits you
So cast all your frustrations to the bottomless sea

I gotta get on
Gotta get on out
All these worried troubled thoughts gotta get on out of my head
Gotta get on out of my head

"NEW WORLD"

I don't remember how the song "New World" came to me, but it's built out of some distinct memories of being in the woods in Minnesota, and how much that is just part of who I am. This song is another one that has those senti-ments of "get up, get out, and do something about it." You can't change where you're from, but you can change where you're going.

Lives in a little lonely town
No one's around, except for the drinking
Nobody ever gets around
But those who leave, the township sinking
May you rot in heaven
Gotta be home by seven

And the field burns away
The sky breathes it in
So why sit and wait for the new world to begin?

I'm coming out across your border
With new orders for you to take
I'd really like to take out your daughter
Down in the water, down by the lake
When the cold water's on her skin
I can feel how long it's been

And the neighbors will all be there
And no one will know what to wear
So why sit and wait for the new world to begin?

I got a lot I gotta do
Just to get through the end of the day
It hardly ever even happens
But I go to sleep the same anyway

And you can't believe in yourself
You can't believe in anyone else
So why sit and wait for the new world to begin?

"APRIL FOOL"

"April Fool" is one of those songs that I didn't have the crucial last little lyric that I needed to finish it. I remember being at the Gramercy Park Hotel in New York, just staring out the window and racking my brain trying to figure out how to finish it. Wondering what magical words were going to be the icing on the cake. Oddly, "won't you be my fashion victim" were those words. I was in New York City.

I was born in April. And pranks are sort of part of the touring life, as people get bored and play jokes on their friends. Trying to be cool is a losing battle. I guess that's kind of the joke.

Quitting after one more last one
Tired of playing the clown
If I want your opinion, I'll ask ya
I can get myself down

Night driving without headlights
Wearing sunglasses too
Looking good, but sure don't feel right
Anything to be cool

Doing hopscotch with my legs tied
Jumping rope in wet cement
Black leather in midday sunshine
All your mother's money's spent

Doing time on the metal detector
I'd like to drown in your pool
Covering up everything that's defective
Anything to be cool

A burning heart
Could be so cool
Won't you be my fashion victim?
Come on, I'm an April fool for you

Holding on to what's left of real life
Anything to be cool

A burning heart
Like an April fool
Won't you be my fashion victim?
Come on, I'm an April fool
I'm a mid-spring snowfall, joke's on you
I'm an April fool for you

I'm an April fool, for you
I'm an April fool

April Fool

Quittin' After one more last one
Tired of being your clown
workin my way up to Alaska
Southern Life's got me down
Doin Hopscotch with my legs tied
Jumpin to Rope in wet cement
Standing out in the fire hydrants
calling old cord cars new dents
Anything to be cool
Fixing up cocktails for my dad's friends
going home when it's light
windin up the keyless horsemen
Riding into the night
night drivin without head lights
wearing sun glasses too

2 years later

Anything to be cool
Doin time on the metal detector
tryin' to get underground
Crowerin everything that's deffective
Buyin' time by the pound
Holdin on to whats left of real life.
Holdin up the store Riding into the night
Holdin out for the score maybe the last time
Holdin out for the score move

women you Hate them madly
to win Best Friends

WITHOUT A TRACE

G   Am

I fell in love with a hooker
~~and~~ she laughed in my face
So Seriously I took her
I was a disgrace
I was out of line out of ~~p~~   G
out of time ~~time tr~~ to save face
See the open mouth of my suit
telling ~~my~~ me what a waste
saying leave without a trace
I tried to get a good job
with honest pay   I hear the p
I mine as well join the
I mine as well play drive
Standing in the sun with a pop
Everything is possible
with a lot of luck and a prett
No opinion and no taste AND
leave without a trace
I tried to dance at a funera
New-Oreans style
He made me join with a s
I hade to go file   I joined the grave
Trying to to the right thing
Playin it straight
He right thing changes from state to
And if you go out in your
Don't forget to take your mac
I miss miss your body miss y
and you left without a trace

"WITHOUT A TRACE"

"Without a Trace" is a song about people leaving. Sometimes they come back, and sometimes they don't. It always evokes memories of the first friend I made on the road. She was a young rock and roll kid from the state of Washington. Her name was Friday. Like too many people from the music scene, she died very young. It was drug related and it really threw me for a loop. She had always been there whenever we played the West Coast. She later started her own band and I thought that was great, and then she died.

The song's verses are sort of three vignettes. The first verse is about innocence, the second verse is growing up, and the last verse is mortality. The last verse foreshadows the New Orleans side of me, too, because I had just started visiting there more and more frequently.

Now we dedicate the song to Karl every time we play it.

I fell in love with a hooker
She laughed in my face
So seriously I took her
I was a disgrace
I was out of line, I was out of place
Out of time to save face
See the open mouth of my suitcase?
Saying, "Leave this place"

Leave without a trace

I tried to get a good job
With honest pay
Might as well join the mob
The benefits are okay

Standing in the sun with a popsicle
Everything is possible
With a lot of luck, and a pretty face
And some time to waste

Leave without a trace

I tried to dance at a funeral
New Orleans–style
I joined the Grave Dancers Union
I had to file

Trying to do the right thing; play it straight
The right thing changes from state to state
Don't forget to take your mace
If you're out walking late

I'd like to see your face
You left without a trace
You leave without a trace

"GROWING INTO YOU"

Playing music for a living gives you this unique opportunity to suspend some of the more mundane things about growing up. The anxiety factor is intact in the song, but I'm not afraid of growing up anymore.

You never grow out of mischief making
You never grow out of taking
You never grow out of complicating
When simple things are waiting

But I'm growing into you

There's one thing that I know that's perfectly clear
You never grow out of fear

You never grow out of contemplating
When it ain't worth debating
You never grow out of mistake making
You never grow out of faking

But I'm growing into you

There's one thing that I know that's perfectly clear
You never grow out of fear

I'm growing into you

There's one thing that I know that's perfectly clear
You never grow out of fear

And will I ever, ever, ever get over it?

Get over it

"99%"

The song "99%" came all at once. I had been writing a lot on the acoustic guitar, and I needed to get back to the electric, and this was the result. I just dumped it all onto a four-track one night.

I don't own you
But I know you're mine
Never disown you
Never treat you unkind

But once in a while
You get on my nerves
Once in a while
You get what you deserve
I need you ninety-nine percent of the time
Ninety-nine percent of the time

If I asked you what's on your mind
Would you say me?
Would they be thoughts unkind?

But once in a while
I'm not myself
Once in a while
I think you're someone else
I want you ninety-nine percent of the time
Ninety-nine percent of the time

Let's move in together
Happily ever after

I can't touch you
But you feel so fucking fine
Let's just stay like this
And waste some more time

Once in a while
You get in my way
Once in a while
You know I've got to say
I love you ninety-nine percent of the time
Ninety-nine percent of the time

"THE SUN MAID"

I've always thought it was rebellious and sort of a punk rock move to do
something that was really pretty and the opposite of the loud, fast rule.
      The Sun-Maid raisin box has a woman on it, and I guess I was thinking
about her when I wrote "The Sun Maid." She's the maid of the sun, she's
in charge of keeping it clean—it's a big job. Also, I'd been constantly living
among maids in hotel rooms. Being a man trying to write anthems, of sorts,
for women requires a different approach. I've seen women work very, very
hard and get very, very little in return. I'd hate to clean the sun, you know.

Tell me how you get that shine
You must polish all the time
Though I know your job is thankless
They will thank you up in heaven

The sun maid
Looking for the shade

Though they say she's not too bright
She takes care of all the light
Without you it's cold and stark
We would all be in the dark

Without the sun maid
She never gets paid
Searching for the shade
The sun maid

You are so taken for granted
With each and every seed that's planted
And the earth is so demanding
All the young girls are out tanning

With the sun maid
She's such an old maid
She never gets laid
The sun maid

Now you're tired
Your day is over
Now the moon is one day older

LET YOUR DIM LIGHT SHINE

The success of *Grave Dancers Union* was disorienting. We had no idea what we were getting into. It really showed us the inside of the industry and sent us all over the world in a wider radius than ever before. But I also felt like people were finally understanding what it was that I had to say. It was a little intoxicating. It's like you've been screaming at a wall your entire life, and suddenly the wall decides to listen. My life had gotten so crazy at that point, and I was overwhelmed by the idea of creating something really special.

I'd like to take a moment to talk about my notebooks, which I had been using since high school to jot down notes and lyrics and memories. I managed always to drag spiral notebooks around with me the entire time. It was so hard to keep track of everything while being on the road so much—my socks, my pants, whatever. I actually lost a pair of pants once when I had put them on top of the van to dry out after they got wet during a gig, and I forgot about them and they blew off when we were driving on the freeway. Every now and then, I would lose a notebook, too, and that was a tragedy to me. To me it was always *that* was the notebook that had *the* great song in it—the song that was going to make everyone happy and make us enough money to pay the band and pay the crew.

Some of the outtakes from *Let Your Dim Light Shine* are as good as anything I've ever written, I think. People just wanted hits, and that's not really my bag. These outtakes are recorded somewhere on a cassette tape, or a DAT tape, or some format that probably no one has the machine to play anymore. They're precious to me, but they're outtakes. They're gone.

"MISERY"

I wrote "Misery" in Vancouver. I rented some cheap gear from a local guitar store, and the song just kind of came together. The music that was popular around this time was about depression, and it was deep and honest and had lots of guitars. The song is making fun of people making money off of complaining. Like the blues, it's an expression of desperation. This is our moment to tell people how we really feel. Alternative music finally had a platform, and it was out there, and guitars were king. I miss that and how much raw emotion came out of the rock bands of the eighties and nineties.

They say misery
Loves company
We could start a company
And make misery

Frustrated Incorporated

Well, I know just what you need
I might just have the thing
I know what you pay to see

Put me out of my misery
I'd do it for you, would you do it for me?
We will always be busy
Making misery

We could build a factory
And make misery
We'll create the cure
We made the disease

Frustrated Incorporated

Well, I know just what you need
I might just have the thing
I know what you'd pay to feel

Put me out of my misery
All you suicide kings and you drama queens
Forever after happily
Making misery

Did you satisfy your greed?
Get what you need?
Was it only envy?
So empty

Frustrated Incorporated

"SHUT DOWN"

I suppose the more I was being exposed, or overexposed, the more I feared the attention; I often wanted to just curl up in a ball—to shut down. It's funny to me, too, because I'm writing about writing in this song: "I can write all night, but in the morning I can't read it." I'm talking about my trade and trying so fucking hard to write a good song.

I've been vindicated
I've been loved and hated
I've been pulled aside and told that life was overrated

No, I don't believe it
I just can't conceive it
I can write all night, but in the morning I can't read it

Oh no, don't know what's the matter
Stuck up on a ladder, scared of coming down

If I don't get what I want
And there ain't enough to go around
I become oblivious to the obvious
Just ridiculous

As I flip the pages
You're a time that's ageless
In between us lies a calm before a storm that rages

Thought we were related
Couldn't be separated
Tried to get ahead, but only got decapitated

If I don't get what you want
And you don't get what I need
We become oblivious to the obvious
Just dysfunctional

Shut down, shut down, shut down

When I can't keep from getting down
And I grow tired of hanging 'round
I become invisible, unlivable
Just dysfunctional

Shut down, shut down, shut down

been syndicated I've been syndicated
we pbeen pulled aside and told
that life was overated
to I dont believe it
I just cant concieve it
can fight all night but in the
morning I dont need it · I'll be leavin
I can leave it
Oh no I dont wanna know
drop in dropout   were the time gos
                   just get me to the show
So you think you got it tough rough
its always tough when
good enough is never
good enough

"TO MY OWN DEVICES"

"To My Own Devices" came easy to me. It's kind of a two-chord ramble, extremely economical. It's a very simple song. There was a waitress at the Formosa, a restaurant in West Hollywood, who told us stories about who she'd waited on, people like Elvis. She was great, and I was kind of touched by her conversation with me.

    Vices, whether it's tobacco or drugs or alcohol or whatever—it's a habit. The habit thing for me was just something that most people have to deal with, in some way or another. It's pretty pathetic when it comes right down to it. When left to my own devices, I end up in a restaurant, talking to a waitress who waited on Elvis.

Shouldn'ta got so loaded
I damn near exploded
Oh lord, you know
I should'a known it

Whatever the price is
Whatever the crisis
Oh please, don't leave me
To my own devices

Please don't leave me
To my own devices
Oh please, don't leave me
To my own devices

She was a pretty good waitress
Said she'd waited on Elvis
They said she talks too much

Please don't leave me
To my own devices

Oh please, don't leave me
To my own devices

Save it up for a rainy day
It just rained yesterday

Whatever the price is
Whatever the crisis
Oh please, don't leave me
To my own devices

Please don't leave me
To my own devices
Oh please, don't leave me
To my own devices

She was a pretty good waitress
she said she waited on Elvis
They said she talked too much

And I'm so sad cause I got tired
of being mad but I won't be sad
for long

the roof tore away on the D-C-10
ejected out never to be seen again
until 20 years later in 93
I spotted a skeleton in a tree

"HOPES UP"

Well, "Hopes Up" seems pretty self-explanatory. I was hoping that everything was going to work out. But I still had a philosophy of low expectations. It's not really the idea that things are "too good to be true" or that "everything good must come to an end." It's more the idea that you need to count on yourself and trust your instincts and not just listen to other people telling you that you should be excited about something, because people say a lot of stuff. Dreams can come true, but they usually don't turn out the way people expect. I try to never get my hopes up, and then I'm pleasantly surprised if something turns out right.

There's just no substitute for fun
I've tried every single one
And no one can take your place
Everybody gets replaced

My time has neither come nor gone
It just slips out when I yawn
Without hope I can't go wrong

Don't get my hopes up
Don't get my hopes up
Don't get my hopes up now

It's so hard to settle down
Don't recognize my hometown
Home is where I hang my head
Lost in all these things I said

Been holding my breath for so long
I don't need air anymore
If you never let me breathe
I'll never breathe

Don't get my hopes up
Don't get my hopes up
Don't get my hopes up now

Don't know what I was hoping for
I feel like feeling better than I ever felt before

My time has neither come nor gone
It just slips out when I yawn
Holding my breath for so long
For so long

Don't want to be bored no more
I know there's so much more
Don't know what I was hoping for
I feel like feeling better than I ever felt before

Don't get my hopes up
Don't get my hopes up
Don't get my hopes up now

"BITTERSWEETHEART"

I guess I think I'm pretty clever putting the three words together. It explains something that is either a sweetheart who's bitter or someone with a bitter, sweet heart. Either way, I'm fascinated with the word bittersweet, so I wrote a song about it.

Why you always want to get the best of me
I'm like a seeing-eye dog and I can't even see
They're naked and they're following my master who's blind
And my mind's gone to pieces; I could use some piece of mind

So I picked up the pieces and I made a new start
Stole an old stiletto; started stabbing in the dark
I can't live without it; I would surely fall apart
But it's hard to make arrangements 'round a bittersweetheart

Bittersweetheart, bittersweetheart
Better get yourself a little street smart
Bittersweetheart, sad but true
It's a bittersweetheart that's a hard heart to cure
It's just my bittersweetheart
Bittersweetheart, bittersweetheart

It's like a suicide mission when you can't see no end
Tired of compliment-fishing and impressing your friends
I never kissed no one just to kiss and tell
It's a little bit of heaven and a whole lot of hell

In the eye of the beholder is a beautiful start
But you always seem to end up with a bittersweetheart
There's a darkness looming, but the sun is shining bright
I can live to see the morning if I stay up all night

Bittersweetheart, bittersweetheart
Without a shortcut; without a head start
Bittersweetheart, sad but true
It's a bittersweetheart that's a hard heart to cure
My bittersweetheart, it's the hardest part
Bittersweetheart

Are you in there, are you beating?
Beating me up until I'm bleeding
How much blood can you spare?

Bittersweetheart, bittersweetheart
Thinkin' just a drink might get you to the good part
Lying in bed just a'wondering what to do
It's a bittersweetheart that's a hard heart to cure

In time inside you find you always wind up with a bittersweetheart

"STRING OF PEARLS"

My desire to be a storyteller is something I've been working on my whole life. The pearl in "String of Pearls" connects the characters and ends up where the story starts: on the street. I wrote this song in one sitting, under a staircase.

She swings a string of pearls on the corner
The streetlights reflect the light in the water
The string it snaps, and the pearls go sailing
And they splash, and bounce, and cross the wet street

As she bends to chase the pearls, a car swings 'round the corner
She darts from the eyes of the panic-struck driver
Who's racing to the delivery room
'Cause in the back seat his wife is busting out of her womb

And the sack breaks and out come the Siamese twins
Who grow up to become the first president
With two heads
Are better than one

He puts his heads in his hands, says, "I got to put my heads together
I can become the best president ever
And not just president
Fend for yourself"

He signs his name and takes the blame
For all of the names with no shame
In their beliefs they adjourn and they leave
And in walks a man with a broom and a knife and blood on his hands

And he sweeps everything under the rug
And goes home to his kids and gives them a hug
But his wife was not there, she had just left a letter
That said you'd be much better off without me

Now his wife took the train to her ex-lover's funeral
Who died in the bathroom; hit his head on a urinal
When they got together the knowledge was carnal
And the widow was at the funeral, and they had quite a catfight

And they fell into the hole where the casket was resting
And the preacher just left in the middle of the service
'Cause death was one thing, but women made him nervous
And he ran to his car, and he drove 'round the corner

Then something in the street caught the light in his eye
He pulled over, reached down, and picked up a pearl from the gutter
And he didn't know what to think
Then he brought it home and washed it in the sink

And he gave the pearl to Sister Mary Theresa
Who could not accept it, so she gave it to Lisa
A young prostitute who was missing a pearl
On the necklace that broke late last night

"CRAWL"

When I was first becoming friends with producer Steve Jordan, he and I had the same music publisher. The publisher encouraged us to write a song together. I went to Steve's apartment in Manhattan, and I asked him where something was in relation to his place, and he looked out the window and said it was "just a crawl home from here." I had some musical ideas I was trying to sort out, and we pretty much sorted out the skeleton for "Crawl" and it ended up on the record.

You got me going
So get me out of here
I should be blowing
In someone else's ear

I'm looking forward to looking back
On days like today
Though I wish you would go away
Stay
Won't you stay?

I'm gonna crawl

I never felt better just crawling home
I'm gonna crawl home, crawl all alone
Good to see you, see you later, maybe one more beer
I'm gonna crawl home, crawl home from here

Some respond to pleasure
Some respond to pain
I'm hanging out to dry
In the pouring rain

Victims of temptation
Never can complain
I could use the sensation
You see I can't feel pain

I'm gonna crawl

I never ever said I'd never make it home
It's just a stone's throw, a crawl home
Good to see you, see you later, maybe one more beer
I'm just a crawl home, a crawl home from here

I could use someone
To drag me out of here
I am that someone
It's all become quite clear

Get me out of here

I never felt better just crawling home
I'm gonna crawl home, crawl home alone
Good to see you, see you later, man, and I'm outta here
I'm just a crawl home, a crawl from here

"CAGED RAT"

"Caged Rat" is a tough one. I was spending a lot of time in hotel rooms. The caged rat is me. I had gone from living in a van to living in small spaces, and I missed the cheap rent and the space that you are afforded living in Minneapolis.

Musically, the song is probably something that I'm more interested in than I often admit. It's basically just kind of like prog-punk. I don't know what it is, but I think it's funny. It's sort of a sound experiment, too. I owe our soundman, Eric Pierson, credit for helping me work out the sound collage and playing instruments with me while I was assembling the song.

Why don't you go home and crawl into your hole?
Why don't you go home and spend some time alone?

In the corner
I looked across the room
To the other corner
I knew I'd be there soon

Caged rat!

In the corner
I looked across the room
I knew I'd be there soon
In the corner

Caged rat!

Why don't you go home and crawl into your hole?
Why don't you go home and spend some time alone?

From the corner
I looked across the room
To the other corner
I knew I'd be there soon

Caged rat!

"EYES OF A CHILD"

"Eyes of a Child" is like a series of stories about different individuals, not unlike "String of Pearls." The wonder in all of us is what makes life worth living. When you're a little baby, you're always seeing new things for the first time, and the longer you live, the more precious those subconscious memories become.

She had thirteen kids; each one had thirteen problems
Three uppers, ten downers, just to put up with this
She don't know which children belong to which father
But she loves them all anyway, and they each get a kiss

And the toilet ain't flushing, and the toaster is smoking
The vacuum don't suck, but it needs a new belt
But she saw the world through the eyes of a child
And remembers how good it was, and how good it felt

He picked up the paper from the bitter cold morning
He had just gone to sleep; he had to get up for work
By morning he's a watchman, by night he's a waiter
In the late afternoon he works as a clerk

And he can't pay the doctor bills; he just can't afford the pills
The car's repossessed, and the child support's due
But he saw the world through the eyes of a child
Big problems seem smaller, and old things seem new

She was just six when she turned her first trick
Now she's thirteen and it don't make her sick
And she does lots of crystal, and she owns her own pistol
Got a goldfish named Silver, and a pimp who's named Rick

And some are like customers, and some are like patients
She'd have gone back to school if she'd just had the patience
But she saw the world through the eyes of a child
With none of the nightmares, and nothing to deny

She saw the world through the eyes of a child
Yes, she's seen it all, and she knows they're all lies

"JUST LIKE ANYONE"

A group of my closest friends from Minneapolis would go to a cabin up north, about three and half hours away from the city. It's typical for cabins in the woods up north to have outhouses. Sitting in an outhouse—or in a filthy toilet at CBGB, or a porta potty at an outdoor festival—provides the rare opportunity for me to get away and contemplate my life. Anyhow, "Just Like Anyone" is basically a meditation on having that moment to realize that, although everyone is different, we all poop and pee.

She walks into the outhouse
The cold night breathes into her face
The flies are standing still now
The moon it spills through the place

And she starts wondering what it's like to be liked by everyone
And like everyone, be just like anyone
Who just wants to be so, just like anyone
Just like anyone

She reaches through the darkness
Her fingers touch the porcelain seat
She spins and pulls her pants down
The cold air holds her like a thief

She starts wondering what they mean
Do they just be mean to be mean?
And thinking about the scene
Do they just want to be seen?
Trying not to seem so, just like anyone
Just like anyone

The door comes screeching open
She walks into the evening air
She disappears in the darkness
All's left the faint smell of her hair

She's done wondering what it's like to be liked by everyone
And like everyone, be just like anyone
Who just wants to be so, just like anyone

And wondering what they mean
Do they just mean to be mean?
And thinking about the scene
Do they just want to be seen?
Trying not to seem so, just like anyone
Just like anyone

he Walks into the Outhouse
The Cold Night Breaths into her Face
he Flys are standing still now
The Moon it spills Through the place
And starts wondering what its liked to be
~~like~~ liked by everyone and like everyone
se just like anyone Who just wants to be so
just like Anyone
She reaches through the darkness
her fingers tough the porcelin seat SHORT
She spins and pulls her pants down CUT
he cold air holds her like a thief
And starts wondering what the mean STAR
Do the just mean to be mean
And thinking about the scene
to they just want to be seen

"NOTHING TO WRITE HOME ABOUT"

I suppose "Nothing to Write Home About" is a sad song. To declare that you went on a great mission for the truth and you still don't have anything to tell your mother sounds like a complete defeat. We tend to overcomplicate things; it's the small steps that we sometimes forget.

Dear Mother, what can I say?
It's been so long since I went away
And, yes, I miss the comforts of home
But I guess I'm better off on my own

No one told me people could be so cruel
Nobody told me about any of this in school
Still nobody understands
The things that I don't understand

I've nothing to write home about
Nothing I have figured out
Still I have the same old doubts
Nothing to write home about

Dear John, that ain't my name
I'm just hangin' 'round to take the blame
I'm filled with guilt
I'm filled with shame
Too much, or not enough, it's all the same

And no one wants to talk about the loss
No one wants to talk about the cost
Everyone just looks away
Just like any other day

I've nothing to write home about
Nothing I have figured out
Still I have the same old doubts
Nothing to write home about

Who can teach me how to change my ways?
Who will come and save the day?
Who will tell me what to say?
When there's nothing left to say

Nobody told me about any of this in school
No one told me I'd be taken for a fool
And everyone just looks away
And tries to make it through the day

I've nothing to write home about
Nothing I have figured out
Still I have the same old doubts
Nothing to write home about

"I DID MY BEST"

"I Did My Best" is the closest I've ever come to writing about being on the road. There's about five categories of songs I try to avoid like the plague: dancing, love, sex, partying, and being on the road. But you gotta write about what you know. It's hard for me to think that I'm not resigning in this song.

Holed up in the dressing room
Without a dress
Kneeling at the confessional
With nothing to confess
And I knew all about my surprise party
I was spoiled and depressed
So I acted surprised, and I told lots of lies
Yes, I did my best

Stop the truck at the truck stop
I need something to help me crash
Food stamps, checks, and credit cards
But they only accepted cash
There was sweat beading on my brow
My heart was beating out of my chest
So I stole everything they couldn't give away
Yes, I did my best

And I did the best that I could do
With all the mess that I've been through
What did you expect me to do?
I did my best for you

I was waiting for a chain reaction
With a missing link
Waiting for that trickle down

Forever circling the sink
I was tired of being tired
I could not get no rest
So I kept sleepwalking
And talking in my sleep
Yes, I did my best

And I did the best that I could do
With all the mess that I've been through
What did you expect me to do?
I did my best for you

derstand what it takes to be a man
nderstand I'll never be more than I am
understand all you need is a plan
od or bad all you need is a plan
plan I'll never have
ever tried to be a man
. thats what I am
n a man without a plan
me close Hold me tight Hold me al
old up in the dressing room wit
nothing without a dress
neeling at the confessional wi
nothing to confess
nd I knew all about my su
I was spoiled and depressed
But I acted suprised and I tol
yes I did my best
I was playing the sex symbol
but I just wanted to cra
Food stamps checks and c
but they only accepted
Sweat was beading on my
My heart was beating ou
So I stole everything th
give away yes, I did

waiting tottally killer
for a chain reaction with a m
busy link
waiting for that trickle down foreve
circling the chain in the sink
I was tired of been tired and I
could not get no rest
But I kept sleep walking and talking
in my sleep yes I did my best
That guy looks at himself everday
He knows what he does he deals with himself
Hes behind himself and be side himself
and he don't realy care anyway
cause a job is a job and we give ourselves up
and try not to give ourselves away
but who is it you realy wanna end up wit
at the end of the day
I was hopin I could scam a ride
hopin you wouldn't skin my hide
I DID THE BEST
THAT I COULD
DO WITH ALL THE MASS
I BEEN THROUGH
ME TO DO WHAT DID YOU EXPECT
I DID MY ..

CANDY FROM A STRANGER

O n our seventh record, *Grave Dancers Union*, we were "discovered." Then we had to follow it up, and we came out with *Let Your Dim Light Shine*. And then it was time to follow *that* one up. We were selling millions of records, and I was spending so much time doing show business things, like photo shoots; it really became distracting. I really needed to get back to the music. The thread between what I loved about music and what was being demanded of the band had become lost on me.

So, around this time I decided to move to New Orleans. It seemed like a haven, a sanctuary, a place where music was pure. I also decided to start a trio, called the O'Jeez. I was the drummer, which also helped me get back to my musical rudiments. Kraig Jarret Johnson and Jessy Greene, my closest friends, were the other members of the band. We had so much fun practicing and playing together and being equal songwriters. We all contributed in an equal way, and that was the first time I was involved in anything like that. This, of course, was viewed as a distraction by the people I worked with. The monster that is Soul Asylum had an insatiable appetite for more hits, more press, and more of my time spent away from the writing and the music. I just wanted to play.

The songs on *Candy from a Stranger* were sort of an intense rumination on what success looked like to me. It's a lot of people dangling brass rings in front of you. They want your time because they are trying to make money off you. It's terribly uninspiring.

We went to record *Candy from a Stranger* at a top-notch studio in an industrial park in Miami. The pressure was unmanageable as we were struggling to outdo ourselves.

"CREATURES OF HABIT"

I've always thought good habits were one of the greatest human attributes, right up there with manners. It's just another tune exploring happiness and addiction, and how being addicted to happiness is hopefully a good thing.

If the day wants to begin
You can let the day in
If the darkness has no end
Light up the darkness
It ain't on what you can depend
It's who you can depend on

If the rain wants to come in
You can let the rain in
If the darkness is your friend
You can hold the darkness
And if it ain't what you got
You know you gotta have it
The grass gets greener all the time
For creatures of habit

Look out, here comes one more morning
Habits form without a warning
Love it can be habit-forming

Make your enemies your friends
And leave standing naked
It ain't how much you can take
It's how you take it

Look out, here comes one more morning
Habits form without a warning
Love it can be habit-forming
For creatures of habit

Look out
A habit's forming
It's just one more morning
For creatures of habit

"I WILL STILL BE LAUGHING"

"I Will Still Be Laughing" is about rebellion in the face of doom. I'm owning it and trying to develop a sense of comedy that's going to get me through this.

Doorways open up and close
More ways to a punch line
They're all laughing at your clothes
Standing in the lunch line

You're the talk of the town
First you're up, then you're down
It's a cycle, I've found
It always comes around

But I will still be laughing
Yes, I will still be laughing

Air raids in the afternoon
The children are playing
Switchblades, colored red balloons
No one hears your praying

And it comes back to you
All the things that you do
Will come looking for you
They'll come looking for you

But I will still be laughing
Yes, I will still be laughing

Doorways lead to other rooms
Always leave you lying
Facedown in a stranger's tomb
Didn't know you were dying

You rise and you fall
You wait for the call
You're watching the walls
You're watching the walls

But I will still be laughing

"CLOSE"

Double entendres, metaphors—it's the stuff of songwriting. It's something I do. Each verse of "Close" is describing a different meaning of the word close. I'm always getting closer to understanding, but it's somehow never close enough.

Almost gave up yesterday
Almost made it to the top
Fell short of dying just the other day
Fell short of picking up a mop

If it's the thought that counts, you can always count on me
I think about it all the time
It's gonna hit me like a bolt of white lightning
Here it comes, my peace of mind

'Cause I'm close, so close
I'm close, so close

Falling short of proving it
Just a hair from the truth
Little shy of improving it
But here I come, I'm coming through

Pretty soon I'm gonna shed this skin I'm wearing
I've been keeping it inside
No one cares just how you got there
No one cares how hard you tried

But you're close, so close
You're close, so close

I've known you forever
We complete each other's thoughts
It ain't like we never got in trouble
It's just we've never gotten caught

And if you've got a secret
It's in me you can confide
And if we ever get split up
I'll always be on your side

'Cause we're close, so close
We're close, so close

"SEE YOU LATER"

Someone told me once that I had a fear of abandonment. I don't really know what that means. But missing people and worrying that they're not going to be there when I get back is a big part of what makes me who I am.

I guess I'll see you later
Sweet manipulator
And how I thank you dearly
For helping me see clearly

Yes sir, no sir, let me go sir
I don't even want to know, sir
I've had all that I can take today

But I found out so long ago
It don't matter if it shows
And it's up in the air tonight
Yes, it's up in the air tonight

Now you're anticipating
That nostalgia's waiting
With your social statement
Boxed up in the basement

Yes ma'am, no ma'am, let me go ma'am
I don't even give a damn, ma'am
I suppose I'll stand another day

I booked my flight despite my plans
I hope this flight it never lands
And it's up in the air tonight
Yes, it's up in the air tonight

'Cause I've got all night
To lie here on the floor
I got all night
Just like the night before

So, make it soon
And I guess I'll see you later
I guess I'll see you later

It's so up in the air tonight

"NO TIME FOR WAITING"

I remember when I got the idea for the chorus to "No Time for Waiting."
It's as vivid as if it were yesterday. I had been looking for a way to finish this
song, and I was in New Orleans in my hotel room on St. Charles Avenue.
There was someone else in the room, so I went into the bathroom, shut the
door, and turned on the shower so they couldn't hear what I was doing, and I
began singing the lyrics for the chorus into a dictaphone.

The music of the city was opening my brain, and I loved it. I just wanted
to be there. So in a way, with this song I'm saying that I want to be in New
Orleans. I ain't got time to fuck around with all these other places. At this
point I was committed to New Orleans; I was gonna stay, and I did. New
Orleans is "where the river washes into the sea."

It's enough to make you stay
It's enough to make you go away
But you don't understand how I'm feeling
You don't understand, no, no

It's enough to make you sick
It's enough to make you wanna quit
But you don't understand how I'm feeling
You don't understand my love

It's sad when you can't cry
It all comes down to time keeps flying by
Time keeps telling me

There's no time for waiting
For the river to wash into the sea
And when I reach some understanding
I'm gonna let it wash all over
Wash all over me

It's too much to make you say
That you always want it to be this way
But you don't understand this feeling
So why do I even try?

It's sad when you can't try
It all comes down to time keeps killing time
Time keeps healing

I've no time for waiting
For the river to wash into the sea
And when I reach some understanding
I'm gonna let it wash all over
Wash all over me

But I know one day you'll see
The person I wanted to be
And there's no time for waiting
There's no time for waiting

Can't find the time
There's no time

"LIES OF HATE"

Sterling Campbell, who was our drummer at the time, gave me a ninety-minute cassette tape with a lot of cool ideas. He was humming melodies, which I then turned into words to create "Lies of Hate." Most of the music in this song is Sterling's creation.

You make me fall from
The lies of hate
You make these walls from
The lines on my face

Nobody's watching so why do you act like a fake?

You make me crawl from
The lies of hate
You wake me up from
The lines that separate

And when you shine
I know how to find out about
How to get out of it
How to get out of this chase
How to get out of it
How to get out of this place

You make me fall from
The lies of hate

And when you shine
I know how to find out about
How to get out of it
How to get out of this chase
How to find out about

How to get out of it
How to get out of your space
How to get out of it
How to get out of this place
How to find out about
How to go out without
Living the lies of hate

"DRAGGIN' THE LAKE"

Minnesota is the land of ten thousand lakes. You're never that far from a lake when you're in Minnesota. We would hear stories about people drowning in lakes, and when I was very young, somebody tried to explain to me how they would drag the lakes to find bodies. I pictured it like a large piece of plywood with nails on it; I still don't know what the tool looks like for finding a body on the bottom of a lake. But it made an impression on me. In "Draggin' the Lake," I also reference the Mississippi River, which shows up in a lot of my songs. I went to the river but got dragged into the lake, and then I eventually followed the river all the way down to New Orleans.

Around the time I wrote the song, I also started feeling like I was invisible, facing the general quandary of, does anyone give a shit? Am I still here? I'm still here.

Sent on a mission to find out just how much shit one man can take
Went to the river to swim upstream but got dragged into the lake

You're wide-awake
But still you're dreaming
The pride it takes
It has no meaning

Am I still here?
Can you see me, please say yes
Can you heal me, please say yes
When you watch over me, I am blessed

Now that you're all grown up, you're not so self-assured, you'll never know
Who do you answer to when no one's hanging 'round to let it show?

You're wide-awake
But still you're dreaming
The pride it takes
It has no meaning

Am I still here?
Can you hear me, please say yes
Can you heal me, please say yes
When you watch over me, I am blessed

You're old enough to know better than to expect anything
Take care of yourself; you should know not to depend on anyone

Am I still here?
Can you feel me, please say yes
Can you heal me, please say yes
When you watch over me, I am blessed

"NEW YORK BLACKOUT".

*As a songwriter, you always hope you're going to have an experience that
inspires you to write about it. I lived through a blackout in New York City.
When I was a kid, whenever the power went out in the house, it somehow
brought the family together, lighting candles and such. To see it happen in
Manhattan, on such a large scale, was unbelievable.*

*I'm doing some wordplay again in "New York Blackout," with the power
going out and people having drunken blackouts.*

When you chew my ear off, try and let me know
You will never get another piece of me
'Cause in a New York blackout, things go kinda slow
And you miss the things you never thought you'd see

There's still so many things I want to be
Sometimes I just don't even want to sleep
In a New York blackout, it's so hard to see
All the angels that are looking after me

The lights bounce off the water in your eyes
And the dead lift their heads and come alive

I may never escape this darkened city
Still I'm trying to find you in this blackout

Where it's warm inside and always open late
And the doors to hell look just like heaven's gate
And you never know what's going on inside
'Til you step out of the cold and seal your fate

And you might just stop in and say hello
But you've got much more important places to go
Make sure you let everybody know
And I may never enlight this darkened city
Still I'm trying to find you in this blackout

In a New York blackout, you might think I'm gone
But I'll wake up on the front steps of your door

"THE GAME"

The games people play with each other in relationships is ridiculous to me.

My friend's wife, she plays the game
Plays it with me all the time
Makes me feel pretty good, I guess
Hey, that's a pretty dress

But you shouldn't have
No, you shouldn't have
Let me know
No, you shouldn't have
Really shouldn't have
Let it show

Play with me
Don't play with me, don't play
Don't you want to play the game?

If I were a renegade
And you were the county line
Will I have to cross it now?
I got yours and you got mine

But you shouldn't have
No, you shouldn't have
Let it go

Play with me
Don't play with me, don't play
Don't you want to play the game?

Jealousy is just a game
It ties you up and wraps around your brain
Makes you feel like you might hurt yourself
Makes you feel insane

Play with me
Don't play with me, don't play
Don't you want to play the game?

"CRADLE CHAIN"

Musically, "Cradle Chain" had great potential. Lyrically, it was a bit dark. It was different, but listenable. I started thinking about "Rock-a-bye Baby," the nursery rhyme, and the line "down will come baby, cradle and all." Basically, I think the baby suffers a serious injury at the end of that song. Who the fuck sings that to their kid as their kid's going to bed? That becomes the metaphor of the cradle chain, which becomes a metaphor for the umbilical cord, which becomes a thing about just growing up—taking it on the chin, being a man, whatever you want to call it. I especially like the part in the song about wanting to hear the sound of someone else's breathing. That's a good sound.

It's a shame you're not here
On the cross in my ear
Hearing things loud and clear
Come outside, have no fear

And clear the smoke, get some fresh air
Someone waits, someone cares
In the broad light of day
Trouble seems so far away
At the top of the day when the wind sways

Lose the cradle chain
Give it up, give it a name
The child that remains
Nothing's lost, take these chains
Take them away

Please don't ask me how I am
A little tired, a little scared
I'm not amused, I'm not upset
Don't need a leash, I'm not your pet

So, loosen up, feel the breeze
Let me hear you breathe
It's better than, bitter now
When you breathe, I love that sound
But you know I'll look after you like no one

Lose the cradle chain
Give it up, give it a name
The child that remains
Nothing's lost, take these chains
Take them away

If I die before I wake
Light a fuse, bake a cake
I don't mind if I go
Make it quick, don't be slow
But you know I'll remember you like no one

Lose the cradle chain
Give it up, give it a name
The smile that remains
Will take these chains away

THE SILVER LINING

Right before we started making *The Silver Lining*, we found out Karl Mueller was dying. It both stalled the record and gave it urgency. The songs were written, for the most part, but it was probably the most unsure time in the band's existence. No one knew what was going to happen. We were all just hoping Karl would somehow get through it. I was living full-time in New Orleans, and I had a baby, so a lot was going on.

Some of the record also pertains to Hurricane Katrina. Embracing life in New Orleans and embracing disaster at the same time—it's kind of littered throughout the record, right down to the song "Standing Water" and the lighthouse image on the cover. It was a strange time. Being cast out of your own city is a uniquely tragic experience, more so for people who were born there or had lived there most of their lives than for me. I've never seen anything like it, nor do I ever want to see anything like it again.

It may sound like a strange analogy, but the seeming extinction of the city of New Orleans reflected my fear about the possible extinction of the band and not knowing what would happen with Karl. We really had to group together and fight for the band.

I should also note that Michael Bland joined the band as the drummer for this album, and that really opened up a lot of potential for writing. Suddenly, I felt like I could write anything and it would work because of his ability to channel a song.

When the record was finished, I played it for the mother of my child. She listened and thought it was really good, which seemed like a bad thing to her because if the album did well, it would take me away from my family.

"STAND UP AND BE STRONG"

Eli, my son, wasn't born yet. Karl hadn't been diagnosed with cancer yet. I was in New Orleans, and I needed an anthem. Something to assure myself that I was going to get through whatever comes my way. That's where "Stand Up and Be Strong" came from.

Sometimes I think all my songs are fight songs, and this is a good example—especially when everyone yells "Fight!" when we play it live.

You might be right
You might be wrong
You might just think your life has gone on for too long

Your knees get weak
And your heart grows cold
And you're tired of doing everything you're told

Nothing can take
Away from you
What you take
And what you've been through

Stand up and be strong
Stand up and be strong
It won't take long
You can't go wrong
Stand up and be strong

You might have to fight
You might have to cry
You might have to cry
You might have to fight
Stand up and be strong

If you live in the hills
You take too many pills
If you've lost the thrill
Against your own will
Stand up and be strong

Nothing can take
Away from you
What you take
You know what you've got to do

Stand up and be strong
Stand up and be strong
It won't take long
You can't go wrong
Stand up and be strong

If you get all depressed
When you get undressed
If your life's a mess
Remember you're blessed
Stand up and be strong

Stand up and be strong
Stand up and be strong
It won't take long
You can't go wrong
Stand up and be strong

"LATELY"

"Lately" is the middle song in my war trilogy. The first was "Black Gold," and the third one, "Let's All Kill Each Other," is on the next album, Delayed Reaction. *The last line of "Lately" pertains to the part in war where nobody knows where you are or whether you're dead or alive. I suppose, in that one small sense, being a solider is sort of like being in a band on tour, except we don't have to kill anybody. War is a frivolous monster, and I'm fucking sick of it.*

In the fog lights,
There was tear gas floating through the twilight
And he wondered what life would be like
With a giant screen TV
A fridge full of beer
And a conscience that's clean

See lately,
She'd been thinking about her little tiny baby
And the boy who had gone to defend me
She's a good friend of mine
But I can't take the place of her man anytime

And it won't be long
'Till he's coming home

You gotta bring your soldier home
All those stones have all been thrown
You gotta give a kid a chance to get a look at his kid
And hope he can live with whatever he did

Now meanwhile,
He was reading magazines on the front line
He was trying not to think about her life

And what he might have done
'Cause it seemed like neither one of them
Were having any fun

You see lately,
She'd been acting kinda crazy lately
Oh man, I thought she was gonna hate me
'Cause I couldn't watch her little one
I had so much to do
I was so high strung

And it won't be long
Until Daddy's home

You gotta bring your soldier home
All those stones have all been thrown
You gotta give a kid a chance to get a look at his kid
And hope he can live with whatever he did

Lately, all the hate escapes me
Lately, all the hate just escapes me, lately
So he phoned her,
He said, "Darlin', I'm feeling so alone here
Am I making myself perfectly clear?
That I'm on my way back
Just a couple more missions
And I'll start getting packed"

You gotta bring your soldier home
When all those stones have all been thrown
You gotta give a kid a chance to get a look at his kid
And hope he can live with whatever he did

Lately, I was wondering if she's heard from him lately

"CRAZY MIXED UP WORLD"

I'll never forget the first time I heard my son, Eli, sing "Crazy Mixed Up World" to me. It was especially cool because the first verse was written for him, before he was born, and I was writing about when he grows up.

Now that you're old enough
And all grown now
Trying to act so tough
Here comes a slap right in the face

Branding irons and cattle prods
And cowboys everywhere
Ropes flying through the air
Leaves some kind of funny aftertaste

And when the room gets small
And the streets are filled with fighting
You'll find a way to escape
You'll find a better place

'Cause it's a crazy mixed up world out there
Someone's always got a gun, and it's all about money
You live with loneliness
Or you live with somebody who's crazy
It's just a crazy mixed up world

Jet fighters streak the air
Where they're going nobody seems to care
I guess we'll just wait and watch 'em fade

I don't think much about
The things I thought I just couldn't live without
I live without them every day
And when you just can't handle
One more panhandler

It leaves you wishing for change
A fast car to take you away

It's a crazy mixed up world out there
Someone's always got a gun
And it's all about money
You live with loneliness
Or you live with somebody who's crazy
It's just a crazy mixed up world

So take your shattered faith
And make it just like new
With Krazy Glue and tape
You're gonna need it again someday

You're gonna need it again,
You're gonna need it today

'Cause it's a crazy mixed up world out there
Someone's always got a gun
And it's all about money
You live with loneliness
Or you live with somebody who's crazy
It's just a crazy mixed up world

"ALL IS WELL"

*"All Is Well" is about perspective. One man's heaven is another man's hell.
So good luck.*

Black lights and a disco ball
Got the carpets going wall to wall
Maybe someday
Won't be just one way

Had a dream I was lying in hell
Looked a lot like this hotel
Maybe one day
It won't be just one way

But it's one big maybe
Maybe I'm the one who's crazy
How can I find out, how can I wind up
Trying to be like you?

And all is well in hell
I wish you were here
I'm wishing you well

You know who asked about you?
As far as I can tell
All in all, all is well

A bomb shelter and some cans of food
A gas mask looks good on you
Come and see me
You wouldn't want to be me

I think I injured my funny bone
I'm gonna cry when I get home
Maybe one day
Save it for Sunday

And it's one big maybe
Maybe you're the one who's crazy
How can I find out, how can I wind up
Trying to be like you?

And all is well in hell
I wish you were here
I'm wishing you well

You know who asked about you
As far as I can tell
All in all, all is well

All is well here in hell
I wish you were here
I'm wishing you well
All is well here in hell
I wish you were here

All in all, all is well

"BUS NAMED DESIRE"

At our place in New Orleans, every time a bus went by the whole house would shake. One day I was sitting on the porch and I noticed the marquee on the bus said, "Desire." If you're not familiar with A Streetcar Named Desire, the play captures New Orleans in a way I've never seen any other creative work do. Thus, the "Bus Named Desire."

Calling you from inside the wire
I'm payin' my dues underneath your tires

Standing out in the middle of traffic
Photographing the crash
Waitin' in line with little old ladies
With a bug up my ass

I wanna live in your car
I'm never going too far

Calling you from inside the wire
I'm payin' my dues underneath your tires

Got a hostage situation
Someone's crackin' the whip
Some are puttin' up a fierce resistance
Some are gettin' their kicks

Out of the blue and into the fire
I've got no use for being tired

Calling you from inside the wire
I'm payin' my dues underneath your tires
A bus named desire

Now I'm all alone here waiting
Like I'm buried alive
Gotta crawl my way out maybe
If I plan to survive

Born in a zoo, raised in a cage
What's it to you?
If I break through, anyway

Calling you from inside the wire
I'm payin' my dues underneath your tires
A bus named desire

Standin out in the middle of traffic
photo graphing the crash
waitin in line with little old lady
with a pug up my ass
I wanna Live in your car
2 - gotta hostage situation
someones crackin the whip
some put up a fierce resistance -
- some are leaving tips -
turnin the screws -
+ burnin fires +
I got no use - for feelin tor

born in a zoo -
raised in a cage +
whats it to you If I break through
to the light of day (anyway)
Now I'm all alone here waitin
like I'm buried alive

"WHATCHA NEED"

Want need, need want—it's different for everyone.

He spray-painted his wardrobe black
To make the scene
He special ordered boots and hat
From a magazine

Say hello to the underground
Say hello for me

You make believe the end is coming
You'll believe in don't stop running
And you can have your bullets back
Go back to your shotgun shack
You can scare the daylights out of me
If that's whatcha need

She started dating men in black
And circus freaks
She tied their hands behind their backs
And left them there for weeks

Say hello to your mom and dad
Say hello for me

It's strange to me to hurt somebody
Strange to me that no one's coming
Orchestrating your attack
Disappear and fade to black
You can scare the daylights out of me
If that's whatcha need

The light came crawling through the cracks
And it reminded me
That I forgot to call you back
And that you're mad at me

Well, say hello to your bitter friends
Say hello for me

Take your pills and throw 'em back
Watch yourself fall through the cracks
You could scare the daylights out of me
If that's whatcha need

"STANDING WATER"

New Orleans is below sea level, so every puddle is a mosquito-breeding loca-
tion. There's lots of standing water in that city. The rainbow in the lyrics refers
to the gasoline in the water on the side of the road.

I am also referencing Hurricane Katrina. Hurricane season is an annual
time of dread in New Orleans. There's always a chance that everything will
be washed away.

Down from the mountain
Running wild through the trees
A crystal glimmer
Rolling along so effortlessly

Trickled down from the country
But the city sucked it in and spit it out
Now the gravity pulls you
To the curbside now as it's getting light

And it's too soon, too fast
And that ain't ever gonna last

Standing water
Standing too close to the sun
With your rainbow runoff
You're like a sitting duck waiting for the summer rain to come

I was a lowlife in the highlands
I was barely living up to standards and demands
I had run out of reasons
To let myself believe in anything

I wanted to phone home so many times
But I've never given in; you know dreams never die
Woke up in a cold sweat
I was breathing still; my heart wasn't open yet

Dried out by the hot sun
There's never anywhere to run

It's like standing water
Standing too close to the sun
With your rainbow runoff
You're like a sitting duck waiting for the summer rain to come

Where there once was a country
With champagne rivers running wide
There was free land flying
Out the door in the middle of the night

And they were pushing every button
They were paving their way to the blight
They were breaking laws that they had made themselves
Dictating what's wrong and what's right

So proud, so strong
But that don't mean you're never wrong

It's like standing water
Standing too close to the sun
With your rainbow runoff
You're like a sitting duck waiting for the summer rain to come

"SUCCESS IS NOT SO SWEET"

By this time, we had been around the world and dealt with all the trappings of selling a lot of records and being popular. Success can leave a strange taste in your mouth.

Blood on the sidewalk
Washing down the drain
Rushing around the crime scene
To hide behind the stain
Hide behind the pain

Blue-colored lady
Black eye behind her shades
It's funny how the players
They can't survive the game
I'll survive the game

Rule maker
Dream taker
Numbers on a sheet

The execution
The grand delusion
Success is not so sweet

Damaged for the first time
Who knew it'd be you?
You could try to save me
And I'll try to save you
Try to save you

Dealmaker
Heartbreaker
Numbers on a sheet

The wild confusion
The strange delusion
Success is not so sweet

You want a baby
I know you do
I'll be your baby
And I'll take care of you
I'll take care of you

Widow-maker
Deal breaker
The blood runs down the street

The execution
Conclusion
Success is not so sweet

Dream faker
Pocket shaker
The numbers on a sheet

The execution
The institution
Success is not so sweet

"THE GREAT EXAGGERATOR"

Exaggeration is a trait. It was passed down to me from my mother, and it can be a deal breaker in any argument. You can't win an argument by just making up numbers, so don't try to out-exaggerate me. I can bullshit with the best of them.

Can we not talk about this?
I don't wanna talk about that
So maybe put on some records
And kick back

'Cause I'll blow it way out of proportion
Make it loud beyond distortion
Don't ask me now and please don't ask me later
'Cause I am the great exaggerator
Please don't argue with the great exaggerator

We're so misunderstood
Every little thing's taboo
Sometimes I'm so hard
To talk to

'Cause I'll blow it way out of proportion
Make it loud beyond distortion
My mind is bubbling like a percolator
'Cause I am the great exaggerator
Please don't disagree with the great exaggerator

So can we not talk about this?
I don't wanna talk about that
Maybe turn on the TV
And kick back

'Cause I am the great exaggerator
Don't ask me now and please don't ask me later
'Cause I'll blow it way out of proportion
I'll make it loud beyond distortion
Please don't argue with the great exaggerator

"OXYGEN"

I think we can all agree that air is a good thing. "Oxygen" is just a song about suffocation, and the obvious cure.

Wishing upon a mattress
Falling off the axis
Slipping the stillness
Flipping the bird

I'll walk you home when you're wasted
I can almost taste it
All this oxygen's for you

But it's a couple more volts of shock treatment for you
When a couple more votes of confidence will do
I'll walk you home when you're wasted
I can almost taste it

It's a couple more volts of shock treatment for you
When a couple more votes of confidence will do

Always there to remind you
Before and behind you
It follows you everywhere you go

They may say you're crazy
But it don't even faze me
'Cause you're the sanest one I know

Just a couple more breaths of oxygen will do
They may say you're crazy
Makes you so amazing

But it's a couple more volts of shock treatment for you
When a couple more votes of confidence will do

Just a couple more breaths of oxygen will do
But it's a couple more bills and a couple more pills
And a couple more "Why do you do those things you do?"

Just a couple more volts of shock treatment for you
Just a couple more breaths of oxygen will do
Treatment, treatment for you
Shock treatment for you

That'll do

"GOOD FOR YOU"

What's good for you and what people tell you is good for you can be two very different things. I would sometimes notice that people weren't listening to what I was saying, and they'd just respond, "good for you." In another sense, I'm not the best at taking care of myself. I don't always do what's good for me.

It brings me peace
When you're asleep
Alone together
In a moment that lasts forever

And when you smile
It brings me peace
It's like everything
I ever wanted

And I want so bad to be good for you
I could be good for you
I think I'd be good for you
Yes, I think I'd be good for you

Just like orange juice,
Or a walk around the lake
Like putting to good use
Something you thought was fake

And the afterlife
Who really cares
This one's good enough
Just as long as you're there

And I want so bad to be good for you
I could be good for you
I think I'd be good for you
Yes, I could be good for you

And what is sacred
This I know
It's just me and you
On a train moving slow
To Heaven

It's just like my momma
She used to say
When I told her
That everything's okay

She'd just say, "Good for you
That's so good for you
That's good for you
I think it'd be good for you"

Yeah, I think I'd be good for you
I could be good for you
I think I could
I could be good for you

Yes, I think I'd be good for you

"SLOWLY RISING"

Believe it or not, "Slowly Rising" is about women's empowerment.
Every woman's got an arsenal, and you better hope she doesn't use it.
I used the expression "weapons of mass destruction" in the song because
George W. Bush and his cronies were using it ad nauseam—it was
just an excuse to start a war.

She don't need an introduction
She ain't gonna stop production
She's gonna make you feel her suction
She's got the weapons of mass destruction

She's solar powered
She's never saying anything
And the sun shines out of her everywhere

She sees best without her glasses
She does well in all her classes
A cheek for your lips and a cheek for the masses
She's got weapons
She's got weapons

It's so strange
You don't change

Slowly rising

She's solar powered
She's never saying anything
And the sun shines out of her everywhere

He's got the money and you can't have it
She's got the power and he's got the habit
She's gonna make you feel her posture
She's got weapons
She's got weapons

It's so strange
You don't change

Slowly rising

She's solar powered
She's never saying anything
And the sun shines out of her everywhere

"FEARLESS LEADER"

I'm fascinated with the men and women who wield power. Why people designate power to certain individuals is very interesting to me. We all have different perceptions of who people are or were, and whether they were real or not in some cases.

Jesus was a hippie; peace and love was all he was about
That's why they killed him, 'cause that shit's
Something people can't figure out
Now some folks who worship him are the ones
Who would have cheered at the crucifixion
They got no conviction; it doesn't matter if the man was fact or fiction

Nixon was a liar; it's the one thing believed to be true
But Tricky Dick was not a crook, whatever that means,
Whatever presidents do
Money can't buy you children, and nothing can bring them back to you
We all make mistakes; we all need someone to look up to

Who're you gonna call your fearless leader?
Who's gonna put your fears to bed?
Heroes will never let you down just as long as they're dead

Satan is a feeling; deviance, it lurks in everyone
Guilty pleasures and mischievous behavior can be fun
But no one made you do it; nobody but yourself to blame
It's always at your door and trouble is its name

Who're you gonna call your fearless leader?
Who's gonna put your fears to bed?
Heroes will never let you down just as long as they're dead

Sometimes you gotta pick and choose
Sometimes no matter what you lose

Divine was a woman; her private parts they said she was a man
But those were his private parts, the parts that he could never understand
But she was an actress; she could be anything that she wanted
Her reality was the very thing that she flaunted

Who're you gonna call your fearless leader?
Who's gonna put your fears to bed?
Heroes will never let you down just as long as they're dead

Who are you gonna call your fearless leader?
When you run from fear you leave yourself behind
You can't dump your fears on someone else
'Cause it's all in your mind

Jesus was a hippie, peace and love was all he was about
thats why they killed him, that shits something people can't figure out
Now the folks that worship him are the ones who woulda cheered at the crucifixion
they got no conviction it don't matter if the man was fact or fiction
Nixon was a Liar its the one thing believed to be true
But tricky dick was not a crook whatever that means whatever they do
Money can't buy you children nothing can bring them back to you
We all make mistakes we all need someone to look up to
Who you gonna call your fearless leader
whos gonna put your fears to bed
Heros will never let you down
Just as long as their dead
But wait I just found out somethin about someone
who had died died many years ago
That certain someone was not who I thought he was
But I believed in him he was my hero
And I just felt like a sucker I guess you could say he let me down
Its hard to believe in anything the first time around
Sometimes you gotta pick and choose
Sometimes no matter what you lose
Satan is a feeling devience it lurks in everyone
Guilty pleasures mischievous behavior can be fun
No one made you do it nobody but yourself to blame
Its always at your door and trouble is its name
Divine was a woman his private parts they said he was a man
These where her private parts the parts that she could never understand
She was an actress she could be anything that she wanted
and her reality was the very the that she flaunted
who you would your fearless leader
when you run from fear you leave your self behind
You can't dump your fear on someone else
cause its all in your mind

DELAYED REACTION

B y the time we were working on *Delayed Reaction*, I was entrenched in New Orleans culture, and I was very comfortable being there, soaking up the music. That's probably reflected on *Delayed Reaction* more than any other record. I was exploring some of the reasons why I was so attracted to New Orleans music: it was celebratory. I was coming from a punk rock world that's mean and aggressive and full of vitriol. The more I noticed New Orleans musicians smiling and laughing while they played, the more I wanted to be like that.

That's where the rhythms, the polyrhythms, and the syncopation on the record come in. I couldn't have done all that in the past because the band didn't have it in them. But with Michael Bland on drums I was free to explore these rhythms that were so inspiring to me. I always thought about it as, not co-opting, and not necessarily being influenced, but more taking the spirit and bringing it into the music.

I was feeling so connected to the city of New Orleans and so lost at the same time. I was a rock guy in a jazz town; I was a Yankee in the South. I was feeling things that reinforced my alienation and, at the same time, upped my curiosity to go out and find new things, new sounds, and new ways to think about music. To me, jazz music is often more innovative than rock. You can mix all these things together, sort of like New Orleans gumbo. So many different kinds of music came together in this city, and what we know of American music is so rooted in that space. New Orleans has a precious lineage of music.

I was able to find my own musical identity by coming to understand that rock and roll came from many of the same traditions as the street parade music of New Orleans. It was very organic and obvious to me, and it might not have been to other people. I had seen how punk rock was inclusive; the whole idea is that the people onstage are not that different from the people in the audience. That's what you see in a street parade. Sometimes it's hard to distinguish who's in the band and who's not. Everybody's just shakin' a tambourine or whatever.

The title of the record, *Delayed Reaction*, seemed appropriate for what I was going through. You figure out a lot of stuff over the course of your life. You can miss something seemingly obvious for years and then all of a sudden fall into understanding. I see it all the time—"Oh, holy shit, I didn't realize that was connected to this!" Things are interconnected in ways you just don't see when you're younger. It takes a lifetime to sort shit out. It usually comes after you learn more about what it is that you're trying to understand.

"GRAVITY"

When I was a kid, I learned about gravity from the space program. The idea of floating away is dreamlike to me—all the weight taken off your shoulders, and you're just drifting. Weightlessness is like a relief. On the more practical side, the song "Gravity" is also just complaining about having your feet stuck to the ground and not being able to fly.

There's a little man who can get his hands
On a plan to sell the planet
He walks the walk, and he talks the talk
And for half up front you can have it

For every answer there are ways to shoot it down
We'll need some greenbacks, and a green light
Some jets with wings to get this new thing off the ground

But I can't stand the gravity; can't stand it
The way you handle it; I got to hand it to you
No, I can't stand the gravity; can't stand it
Just like you planned it; I'm coming out of my shoes

All shined up, they wind me up
Like a toy on the first day of school
Stranded, abandoned
Still waiting in a line of fools

For every question there are answers to spare
Stop at the convenient store without convenience
We ain't going anywhere

No, I can't stand the gravity; can't stand it
The way you handle it; I got to hand it to you
No, I can't stand the gravity; can't stand it
Just like you planned it; I'm coming out of my shoes

I'm so far from home
Just drifting off alone
Floating away
Off into space

Shine down a dead-end street
Go get what you need
Just a trick or treat
It's all the same to me
Live how you wanna live

Just like a candlelight
Like a shooting star
Still flickering, still glowing
The room is still on fire

For every question there are ways to shoot it down
Put your feet down on the cold ground
I do believe that this time you are coming 'round

I can't stand the gravity; can't stand it
The way you handle it; I got to hand it to you
No, I can't stand the gravity; can't stand it
Just like you planned it; I'm coming out of my shoes

No, I can't stand the gravity; I can't stand it
The way you handle it; I got to hand it to you
No, I can't stand the gravity; I can't stand it
Don't understand it; I'm coming out of my shoes

Shine down a dead-end street
Go get what you need
Just a trick or treat
It's all the same to me
Live how you wanna live
Like a candlelight
Like a shooting star, still flickering

You can always take your time
Unless the room's on fire
Make it last awhile; still glowing
Floating on a summer breeze
In a warm wind, roaring
Like a dandelion starting to disintegrate

"INTO THE LIGHT"

The idea of breaking a horse sounds traumatizing. It's making something that's wild not wild anymore, making a wild animal obedient. That's a big deal in punk music. You don't want to be reined in; you want to be a wild horse; you want to be unleashed. It's another threshold: untamed to tame. I don't know if breaking horses translates that well, but that's what I'm talking about in "Into the Light."

I suppose there's also an element of "there's no going back." Once you've committed yourself to the "life," you're just another horse in the rodeo— and this isn't my first rodeo.

Once you've rolled the dice, you can't think twice
'Cause you would never take your own advice
You're skating on a grave that's paved with ice
You step into the light

I want to be sure this is a sure thing
Not some tangled-up puppeteer's strings
Once you've crossed the line
Stepping into—

Breaking horses, raising Cain
Headed for the hills
The best day ever just got better
It gets better still

So, if you're out tonight, pick me up
Everybody hates being alone
Take me to a place that no one knows
Step into the light

How can I be sure this is a sure thing?
Not some puppet on a string

'Cause once you've crossed the line
You're chasing out the light

Breaking horses, raising Cain
Headed for the hills
The best day ever just got better
It gets better still

So, if you're out tonight, pick me up
You're running out on—

Chasing sirens, red lights change
No time left to kill
Waving flags of fine-drawn lines
Find a cheaper thrill

I want to be sure, this is a sure thing
Because once you've drawn the line
You step into the light
Step into the light

Breaking horses, raising Cain
Headed for the hills
The best day ever just got better
It gets better still

Waving flags of fine-drawn lines
Lines drawn in the sand

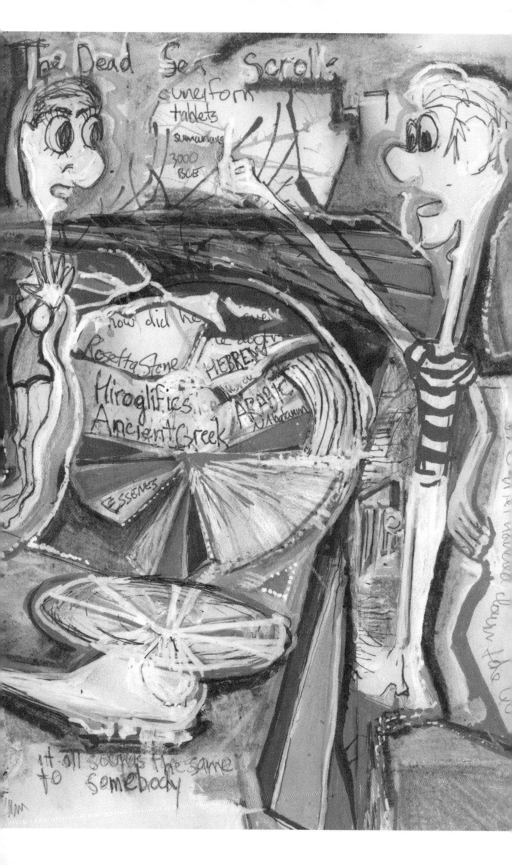

"THE STREETS"

"The Streets" was written in one sitting and sung in one take. There's nothing more satisfying to me than walking into the studio, singing something once, and having this sort of stunned silence coming from the control room like, "Holy shit. What just happened?"

The song explores how to distinguish the virtue of being domesticated from the stigma of being a homeless person. It's always been a fine line with me. I don't want to lose contact with the man on the street or the woman on the bus.

It's never quite complete
It's never ever discrete
People just disappear
And then there's people you meet
They come from everywhere
But not just anywhere
They all got stories to tell
They all got secrets to keep

Then you find someone you like
And maybe go get a bite
Start to feel secure
You think it's something you like
But as you're passing by
You kinda wanna cry
You think that maybe she even
Saved your life

She keeps me off the streets

So, I was shooting the shit
Like I could handle it
Like I could live on the dole

Running around trading bikes
And go and crawl in a hole
When it gets too cold
With nowhere to be, and nowhere to go

No boss to call my own
I'm just wettin' a line
My time is mine; it'd be so divine
Then you meet someone
That seems to know the ropes
Knows how to cheat a con
And knows that life's a joke

She keeps me off the streets

Then you bend the law
And it finally breaks
It breaks over your head
And leaves you in its wake
Then she calls her dad
And lies about the cash
And then she bails you out
Makes you feel like an ass

Where have you gone?
You've been gone for so long
I hear you callin' yourself a vagabond
You're livin' out on the lam
Got yourself in a jam
You got nothing to eat
When I see you again
I'll see you on the street

She keeps me off the streets

"BY THE WAY"

"By the Way" was written for Grave Dancers Union, *actually. It's one of those outtakes that just lingered, and people kept bringing it up. The people in the band and people who listened to the band seemed to remember it from somewhere. I suppose they had heard it from live acoustic performances. It's nice when something that had seemed to be forgotten finally sees the light of day.*

The song melds punk rock dissonance with romantic sentiment. I'm just that guy: "Oh, by the way, I really dig you, but I gotta go. Perhaps I'll be back. Remember me, please."

If I could remember what makes me feel good
I'd pound it down like a nail in wood
I'd never let go of that feeling again, I know

I know that I felt that way before
I'd pound it down like a cellar door
I want you to know I'm behind you, by the way

By the way that you look when I confront you
By the way that I affect the things you do
By the way did I tell you, I can't leave you?
By the way

I'll be waiting for you on judgment day
To watch all these judgments pass away
By the way the details fall, by the way

By the way all the people who care about you
Are all watching to see what you're gonna do
By the way have I told you, I can't leave you?
By the way

By the way that you build me up again
Back to a time when I wasn't so tense
By the way did I tell you, you pay for what you play?

By the way that you make me feel all right
By the way that you put up such a fight
By the way that my trust and faith is safe with you

felt that way before, pound it down like a cedarded
want you know I'm behind you
y the way
the way that ~~I effect~~ you look when I confront
the way that I effect all the things you do
the way did I tell you I cant leave you by the
ll be waiting for you on judgement day
to watch all these judgements pass away
by the way the details fall by the way
by the all the people that care about you, r all watching to see what your gonna
y the way that you build me up again by the way did I tell you
 back to a time ~~that it was not~~ when it all made sense tense
Now I know that you pay for what you play
by the way that you make me feel alright
by the way that you put up such a fight
by the way that my trust and faith
is safe with you

"PIPE DREAM"

It'd be easy to assume I'm talking about crack pipes or whatever in "Pipe Dream," but mostly it's about the audacity of giving up your life to being in a rock band and thinking it's going to work. More often than not, it's just a pipe dream.

I'm all alone
The show's over
Night crawlers crawling closer
Somewhere is temptation
Could it just be my imagination?

Was it all just a dream
At the bottom of a glass?
Next time don't wake me up
All this too must pass

Call me up when you find out what life means
Does it hide in the fire of a smoke screen?
Like a match burning fast in the cold breeze
Like a house made of glass in a pipe dream

Even so, it gets harder
Can't finish what you can't get started
Everywhere seems so broke down
Signs of life are happening anyhow

Should I just disappear
Behind a one-way glass
Remain invisible
All this too must pass

So, call me up when you find out what life means
Does it hide in the fire of a smoke screen?
Like a match burning fast in the cold breeze
Like a house made of glass in a pipe dream

Late at night when I can't sleep
Listen down to the sound on the street
Then the dawn; the dawn comes chasing
To remind me of the time I'm wasting

So, call me up when you find out what life means
Does it hide in the fire of a smoke screen?
Like a match burning fast in the cold breeze
Like a house made of glass in a pipe dream

"LET'S ALL KILL EACH OTHER"

I've already talked about the war trilogy, which began with "Black Gold"
(from Grave Dancers Union) and "Lately" (from The Silver Lining);
"Let's All Kill Each Other" is the final installment. I'm a bit of a pacifist, and
war bothers me to no end. I hate it. It's ridiculous. So the idea of just throwing
up your hands and saying, "Aw, fuck it, let's all just fucking kill each other,"
seems like the only thing that people can come up with. It's just sad. Escala-
tion means obliteration means idiocracy.

I've been reading everything
The papers and the magazines
Believin' every word I read

Way too many mouths to feed
But we can all agree on greed
And everybody's better off dead

If you're lookin' for some inspiration
Passed on through the generation

Let's all kill each other
Kill your sisters and kill your brothers
Take the fun out of one another
Let's all kill each other

I'm not having any fun
I'm sick and tired of everyone
I wonder what's the right thing to do

Knives and guns for everyone
Now everyone protect someone
At least that's what I learned from you

Just can't trust anyone else
Gonna have to do it ourselves

Let's all kill each other
Kill your fathers and kill your mothers
Take the life out of one another
Let's all kill each other

Let's all kill each other
Kill your sisters and kill your brothers
Take the fun out of one another
Let's all kill each other

Maybe we could talk it out
Maybe I could shout you down

Everything's so complicated
I can't believe how long we've waited
We can try to figure it out
I know what to do about it

Let's all kill each other

If you're looking for a little reaction
Here comes your coming attraction

Let's all kill each other
Kill your sisters and kill your brothers
Take the fun out of one another
Let's all kill each other

Let's all kill each other
Kill your fathers and kill your mothers
Take the life out of one another
Let's all kill each other

"CRUEL INTENTIONS"

In New Orleans, I would go to the clubs and listen to jazz and try to better understand the things I loved about jazz music. An idea kept coming around to me, and it turned out to be "Cruel Intentions." I worked relentlessly on it on the piano. The song came out of listening to a lot of jazz music.

I'm an amateur piano player at best. But just being in New Orleans and listening gave me the ability to understand the instrument in a way that allowed me to at least play my own version of what I was hearing. "Cruel Intentions" is me pretending to be a jazz pianist and a lounge singer and other things in music that I love but will never be. Every now and then I get to take a shot at something I probably shouldn't be doing but I enjoy doing anyway. If I get away with it, I'll never really know.

Cruel intentions, harbored for thee
Too few to mention, but not too hard to see
Shrewd inventions and mysterious schemes
I need prevention
Do you see that it's true?
All you care about is you
And maybe that's cruel
So, save your cruel intentions for somebody other than me

Sweet pretentions, so cute and in style
Sales potential, yes, I'd walk a mile
Unholy places and so much to see
I need a replacement now
Do you see that it's true
Your whole world spins 'round you
And maybe that's cruel
So, save your cruel intentions for somebody other than me

Cruel intentions, harbored for thee
Too few to mention, but do you see that it's true?
Your whole world spins 'round you
And maybe that's cruel
So, save your cruel intentions for somebody other than me

"THE JUICE"

I don't remember when I learned what it means for someone to have "juice."
It's basically confidence or empowerment or, you know, something that gets
you into a club, for example. It's kind of like when you tell somebody you love
them and you don't know if they'll say it back and it's just hanging there.
And then they respond, and say, "I love you too," and you feel invincible—
you got juice.

It was the day after vacation
Heading back to school
Roll over, say goodbye
And whisper, "I love you"

It floated up around the room
And drifted towards the door
Then the phone rang; the mailman came
Left me wanting more

Sometimes it just hangs in the air
Like a crime without a clue
But just like that, you got me back
And you said, "I love you too"

I got my "I love you too"
I got my "I love you too"
I'm gonna squeeze it right out of you
That's when I know I got the juice

We both stared at the ceiling
There's always work to do
With all these mixed-up feelings
Floatin' 'round the room

Like a lost echo hanging in the hills
Trying to find its way back home
Closer and closer
Like a skippin' stone

I got my "I love you too"
I got my "I love you too"
Well, it's all I ever wanted from you
That's when I know I got the juice

Later on that evening
Around the time I get so tense
The rooms seem like cages
The walls seem like a fence

I got my "I love you too"
Yes, I got my "I love you too"
And the whole wide world is waiting for you
For you to say, "I love you too"

"TAKE MANHATTAN"

Songs like "Take Manhattan" are a rare accomplishment as far as I'm concerned. It's telling a story. It's fast, it rocks hard, and there's a lot going on, which is a goal I've always strived for—to fit all that into a song. It's a little like "The Streets" in that it's very fast and telling a story in the vein of Bob Dylan's "Tangled Up in Blue," which is probably one of my favorite songs ever. "Take Manhattan" is about two people who meet at the airport, which I turned into this thing about the Mississippi River and about the North and the South. A lot of my experience at that point had been talking to travelers—people at airports, people on buses, wherever—and it had an effect on me as I decided that I didn't want to live on the East Coast or the West Coast, and the Mississippi was where I belonged.

Well, she started out working for an Illinois assembly line
Not really what she wanted
Just dealing with the feeling when you're feeling like you wish it was fine
You just don't talk about it

Then along came an offer from the city of steel
They were stranded at the airport
She could barely believe he was real

So, she said,
Make it happen, take me to Manhattan
If you like LA, that's cool
Or you can slip me right on down the Mississippi
I'd go anywhere with you

Well, they met up on the river in the middle of the summertime
He was from out on the coast
And ever since he said he'd never stop until they got it right
It's what they wanted the most
He had been everywhere, and she'd been alone
They were just looking for a place to call home

So, he said,
How 'bout Manhattan, we could make it happen
I'll do California too
I know it's iffy, but how 'bout the Mississippi
I'd go anywhere with you

Any old town will do
I could die in the flyover zone with you

Then they started their first argument, and then the fighting never stopped
It's just the same old story
All the boys and girls who never figure one another out
Then all the tears start pouring

She never wanted to see him again
Then the map came off the wall
She started marking with a red pen

Then she said,
Take Manhattan, where anything can happen
You take California too
Forever after, with or without laughter
We got better things to do

Take Manhattan, where anything can happen
You take California too
Take the planet, you can fucking have it
Look out 'cause she's coming for you

"I SHOULD'VE STAYED IN BED"

"I Should've Stayed in Bed" was written a couple of years earlier. I very distinctly remember writing it. I suppose the song comes from the idea that the moment I get out of bed and start doing stuff, I feel like I'm going to fuck everything up. So, what's the point of even getting up?

"I Should've Stayed in Bed" was written around the same time as "By the Way." Dan Murphy really wanted this song, and that song, on the record, and I was pleased it was finally going to happen. It was an opportunity for me to get string players and hear the concept that I've always heard in my head. The song is extremely passive, and that's kind of the funny part to me. It's very existential—the idea that doing nothing might be a better move than doing something. But, you know, you might miss out on life if you don't get the fuck out of bed.

I'm gonna stay in bed all day
I'm gonna stay in bed all day
But this could be my lucky day
Or it could turn to black
I might get lucky anyway
I might never come back

And it's too late for a wake-up call
Too late for a wake-up call

I'm gonna put it off today
I'm gonna put you on
There's nothing I got to do today
Except for blow you off
My dreams are all just throwaways
My superstitions lack
I'm just unlucky anyway
All of my cats are black

Don't let the sun pass you by
Don't let it fall from the sky
Don't let the sunshine pass you by
Don't let the tear fall from your eye

I coulda stayed in bed all day
I coulda stayed in bed all day
Nothing I got to do today
I might just rise and shine

Don't let the sun pass you by
Don't let it fall from the sky
Don't let the sunshine pass you by
Don't let the tear fall from your eye

It's there each time I turn around
I look away and you'll be gone
I could have done so many things
I could've stayed
I should've stayed

I should've stayed in bed all day
I should've stayed in bed

I could a put it off today
I should of put you on
I couldn put you on today
I could put it off

SOUL ASYLUM   CHANGE OF FORTUNE

CHANGE OF FORTUNE

When I was writing *Change of Fortune*, I was still immersed in the music and culture of New Orleans, but I was gradually coming back to Minneapolis. I didn't realize it at the time. I was mostly holed up alone in my studio in New Orleans writing, and I would bring ideas back to Minneapolis and play through them with the band. Syncopation and rhythms and broadening my perspective on what can be done with music—these factors were in full force. I was comfortable playing everything myself, making and fleshing out demos, and basically being isolated. The town that had such a communal connection for me was slipping into the background. I was focused on my music and my kid. At times it even seemed like it was almost balanced. After he went to bed, I went to the studio and pretty much stayed there until the next morning.

In New Orleans I had found my mecca. To me, it's the center of American music, and everyone should go there to experience those musical traditions. I learned so much, and that will always be with me. I still think it's the greatest city in the world, but living in New Orleans had started to become alienating for me. It was a very introspective time.

The rest of it's pretty much like a monkey on a cell phone—it's absurd. Here are these incredible musicians playing in New Orleans, barely getting paid, if at all, and then I go on tour and I see a bunch of half-ass musicians making a lot of money. I'd rather listen to people who have mastered the art of their instruments. Hopefully it'll all come to light in the end and people will get recognized accordingly. I can't explain how much knowledge I gained from the musicians of New Orleans, and they're still there, playing almost every night.

"SUPERSONIC"

"Supersonic" is like a call to action, but I'm also talking to myself. It's just a loud, passionate declaration. This song also reflects my getting back into electric music after being immersed in acoustic music.

Call me at the office
Call me sad but true
It calms me when you call me
It keeps me in my room

Supersonic just how you want it
Catatonic she's always on it
Supersonic she's always on the way

Automatic autumn
Left it sound and safe
We are moving onward
Wasting away

Supersonic just how you want it
Catatonic she's always on it
Supersonic she's always on the way

Walk through the gates
As they watch you walk by
Then you become someone in and out of line

So meet me at the station
Let's pretend to go somewhere

Supersonic I'm always on it
Catatonic just how you want it
It's so ironic
I'm always on the way

Supersonic just how you want it
Catatonic electro techtronic
New products are always on the way

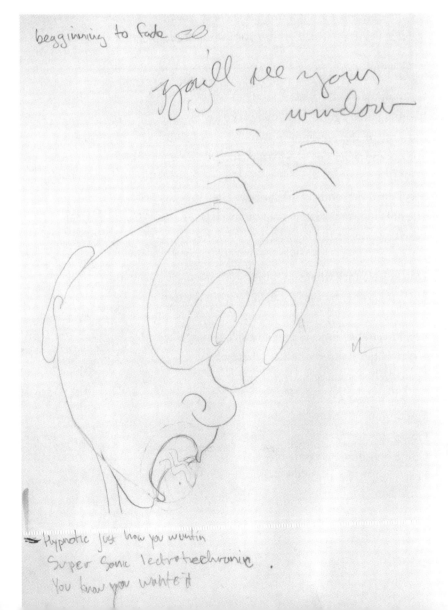

"CAN'T HELP IT"

"Can't Help It" was one of the most exciting studio experiences I've had. I wrote this song on acoustic guitar but was specifically thinking it would sound great electric. I brought it to the studio, and Michael Bland was trying to understand the movement of the riff, and I said, "Think in sixteenth," and suddenly it clicked. Music moves in mysterious ways. Some people can speak in musical terms, and Michael has a more literal background than most. Trying to explain your ideas and concepts to someone else can be tricky. It can be funny, because the untrained folks have to sing their ideas and express their ideas without having the benefit of a musical education.

Got it figured out, I guess
It's going pretty good, but I couldn't care less
Blow me off and shoot me down
You got me right, I'm a goddamn clown

See, I need the kinda help that I can't get anywhere else
She only helps those who help themselves
I can't help myself

Don't give a fuck what you think about me
I'm just another bad apple fallen far from the tree

See, I need the kinda help that I can't get anywhere else
She only helps those who help themselves
I can't help myself

You want it
I'm on it
Come on, come on, come on
I can't help it, I just can't help it

I tried and tried to talk to you
It just don't matter 'cause it just ain't true

See, I need the kinda help that I can't get anywhere else
She only helps those who help themselves
I can't help myself

I can't help it!
I just can't help it!

I can't help myself

"DOOMSDAY"

"Doomsday" is one of those songs I worked on for ten years, give or take. The lyrics finally came together as we were working on Change of Fortune, *and the song is saying what I want to say. It has a timeless "end of the world" sentiment. I don't know why people are so infatuated with the world coming to an end. Personally, I don't think it will happen in my time, even though people seem hell-bent on destroying the planet.*

You don't have to worry about a thing if the end of the world is coming
Just sit back and take it easy 'cause there ain't no use in running
This simple little pamphlet gives you prophets to believe in
And if I had the answers I would still believe, I'd still be leavin'

Hit the ground running
And run before they run you down
Get ready, it's coming
And then another doomsday is done
Another doomsday is done
And I'm hoping that you won't be disappointed
If the end of the world don't come

On the banks of the Mississippi with a radio antenna crack pipe
If I were you and you were me, do you think we could work this out right
It's a simple proposition just to get past this suspicion
And if I had my wishes
I would wade in the wake of the well where you're wishin'

Hit the ground running
And run before they run you down
Get ready, it's coming
And then another doomsday is done
Another doomsday is done
And I'm hoping that you won't be disappointed
If the end of the world don't come

So have a drink and a smoke for me when you get to where you're going
I'll be here just shooting the breeze
Just as long as the wicked wind keeps blowing

Hit the ground running
And run before they run you down
Get ready, it's coming
And then another doomsday is done
Another doomsday is done
And I'm hoping that you won't be disappointed
If the end of the world don't come

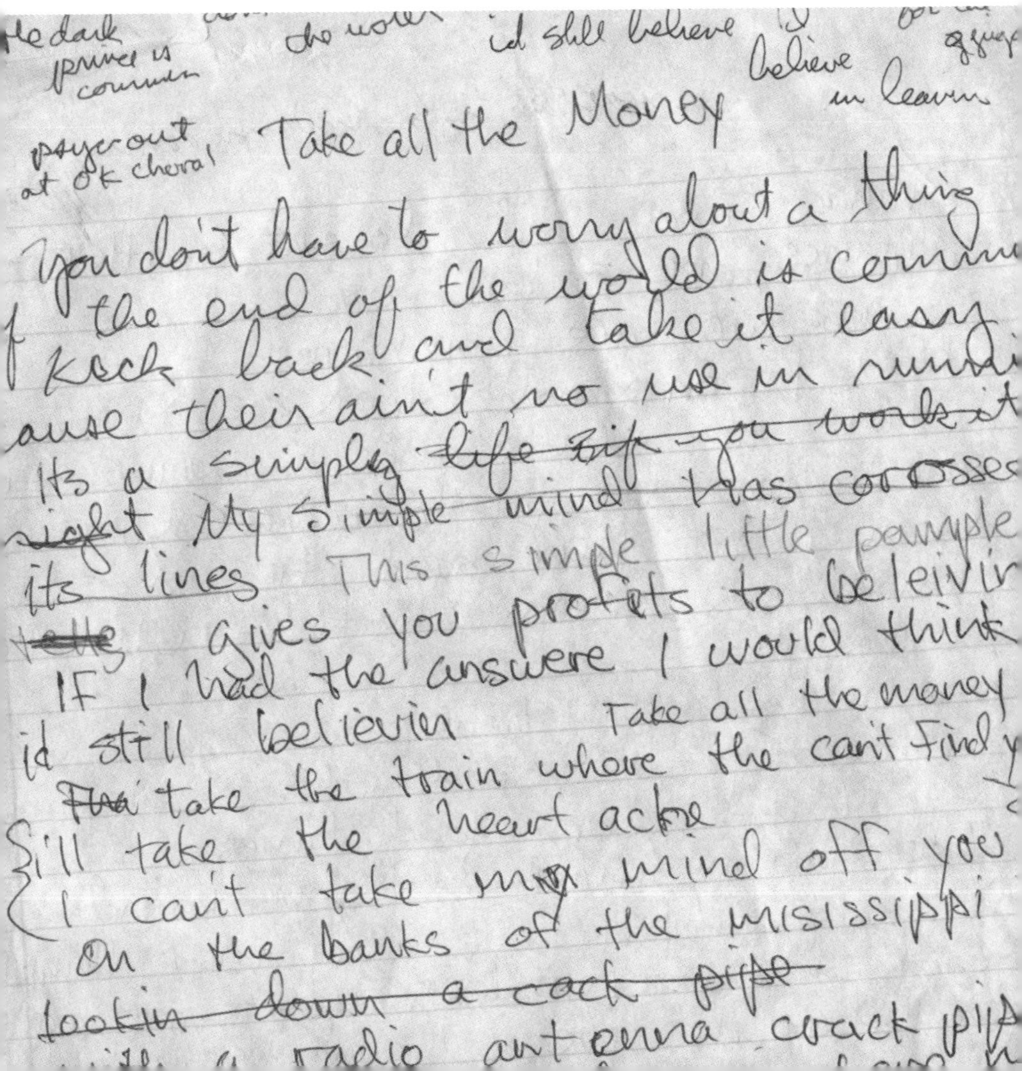

[handwritten notes:]

le dark is coming
prayer out at OK choral

Take all the Money

the world id still believe believe
believe in leavin

You don't have to worry about a thing
f the end of the world is coming
kick back and take it easy
ause their ain't no use in runnin
Its a simply life like you work it
right My simple mind has crosses
its lines This simple little pample
gives you profits to beleivin
IF I had the answere I would think
id still beleivin   Take all the money
that take the train where the can't find y
ill take the heart ache
I can't take my mind off you
On the banks of the misissippi
lookin down a cack pipe
a radio antenna crack pipe

"LADIES MAN"

"Ladies Man" is tongue in cheek. I was talking about someone else. I was comfortable in my marriage. The idea of a fella who has that kind of confidence is alien to me.

As you make your way through the fresh demolition
You better think of something that sounds true
You're the last fighter on the planet
And everyone can see the sadness that's inside of you
Long live exiled isolation

Now, he's a ladies' man
He's a ladies' man
He's a ladies' man
He's a ladies' man

All aboard for an all-expense-paid vacation
This landscape demands an explanation
Pack your bags 'cause we're going to hell
The captain's drinking at the wishing well
Will he ever, ever, really learn

Now, he's a ladies' man
He's a ladies' man
He's a ladies' man
Well, he's a ladies' man

Take it back to the last abomination
Get yourself ready for the ride you've been waiting for
Hot rods and real cool revelations

Yes, he's a ladies' man
Well, he's a ladies' man
And she's a lady, man

Take cover
Take cover
Take cover in the dumpster

Take cover

"MOONSHINE"

"Moonshine" doesn't have anything to do with making your own alcohol. (Although I did go to a benefit in Kentucky once where everyone made their own alcohol and grew their own weed—and I gotta say, I had a pretty good time.) The song is about how the illusion, or delusion, of having fun can be fundamentally at odds with reality. It's about waking up in the morning and wondering if you actually had fun the night before or if you were just high on something, whatever it was. Or maybe you fucked up, got fucked up, and fucked something up.

When it's all said and done, the real work has just begun
And suddenly, no one's around
At the end of the rainbow, there's a hole in the endless road
And the damage is always under control

Take the day away from all those obtuse obligations
You can't take a vacation when there's nowhere left to go
Sink or swim the sharks below a starfish constellation
You can't afford the ticket, and you've got no reservation

Please, have some faith
Lord, save this godforsaken paradise
And you've got your reasons, and I've got mine
Are we having a good time?
Or is it just the moonshine?

Now, if I make it to heaven, and we all get to live together forever
Promise you'll be there
The apocalypse missed us, one more time
Mother Nature kissed us goodbye
But somehow, you're still there

One more crystal castle shattered at its core foundation
They use abbreviation when they've got somewhere to go
Though you know it's artificial, still it's an emotion
And now that it's official, you've got feelings

So please, have some faith
Lord, save this godforsaken paradise
You've got your problems, and I've got mine
Are you having a good time?
Or is it just the moonshine?

There's a whip and a red cape, and a bull, and a plane full of snakes
And the damage I'm looking, looking, looking . . .

Now, you got your story and I've got mine
Are we having a good time?
I've got nothing but time

"MAKE IT REAL"

"Make It Real" seems self-explanatory, at least to me. As pretentious as it might sound, I'm always trying to find the truth in things, what is real as opposed to people's fucked-up construction of what they think is real.

The music in this song is very special and progressive to me. Michael Bland opened a door that I was knocking at for a very long time. A great drummer can bring fluidity to complex composition. It may sound frag-mented and fucked up, but I'm always trying to make songs like "Make It Real" because it's what I really want to do—make fucked-up music that's real.

You know you got an understanding, how to make it better
I shouldn't be so damn demanding, write it down in a letter

You can see what you wanna
Lay it out on the table
Could it be any wronger
Can you hear what I'm saying

How you gonna make it real
How you gonna make it
How you gonna make it
How you gonna make it feel
And we won't look the other way

How long you gonna keep on standing, for this misunderstanding
You know it's all a half-assed scam now, and it's all in your head

You can say what you wanna
Take a spin of the wheel
How you gonna make it real
How you gonna make it
How you gonna make it

How you gonna make it feel
And we won't look the other way

Everything is happening
Everything's virtually happening
Running out of time
Standing in line
Trying to find a way to make it real this time

You know you got an understanding how to make it real

How you gonna make it real
How you gonna make it
How you gonna make it
How you gonna make it feel

How you gonna make it
How you gonna make it

"WHEN I SEE YOU"

The reality of being in a rock band is that if you're doing good, you're on tour. And that means you're away from your wife, or your girlfriend, or your family, or your friends, or whatever it is that you're longing to return to.

When I wrote this song I was living in a practice space in Metairie, Louisiana, which was about thirty-five minutes away from where my son lived. This was a major blow because I wasn't even on tour, and I still couldn't see him, and I missed my son more than anyone can imagine. And that's pretty much what this song is about.

I can see I'm so far away
Can't see it any other way
When it really works, I don't get in the way

Is this a job, is this a joke
I'm breathing fire, you're blowing smoke
I've been blinded by what I know
And all I know

Is when I see you, I wanna be with you
I want you to see the real me

Now what if I get lost on the way
And I say all those things you don't want me to say
What if we're still going the same way

You're not a victim, not in danger
I'm not your rival, not a stranger
I've been blinded by what I know
And all I know

When I see you, I wanna be with you
I want you to see the real me
When I see you, I wanna be with you
I want you to see what's inside of me

No matter what you do or what you say
I don't want you to change, but you can change

When I see you, I wanna be with you
I want you to see the real me
When I see you, I wanna be with you
I want you to see what's inside of me

I want you to be
I want you to be whoever you want to be

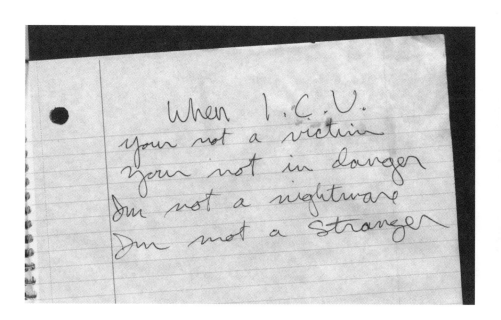

"DEALING"

"Dealing" makes me think about the gifts of the people I am privileged to work with. This song reflects an "anything goes" and "everything goes" situation. Those are my standards, and Michael Bland and producer John Fields allowed me to express myself. "Dealing" was another song that had been around for a while but was ignored until it came out on the record. The song is connected to things that were happening with the band that we were forced to deal with, whether it was the bullshit of the business or just the hassle of surviving.

Everybody knows anything goes
We were only trying to have a good time
Living while you learn, you'll get your turn
We were only living with the one life

When you point the finger, do you often find it pointed back at you?
When you look in the mirror, do you wonder who is looking back at you?

And this is what we're dealing
This is what we're dealing with

Every move you make's like a slithering snake
Winding up the coil to wasting your time
I don't know what you heard; this is absurd
You're trying to set yourself up for last time

When you point the finger, do you often find it pointed back at you?
When you look in the mirror, do you wonder who is looking back at you?

And this is what we're dealing
This is what we're dealing with
And this is what we're dealing
This is what we're dealing with

When you look in the mirror, do you wonder who is looking back at you?
When you point the finger, do you often find it pointed back at you?

And this is what we're dealing
This is what we're dealing with
This is what we're dealing
This is what we're dealing with

"DON'T BOTHER ME"

*In "Don't Bother Me," I'm responding to the notions of "stop bugging me"
and "I don't give a shit." I thought it was funny and interesting. It seems to
work. It's probably not in the right key, though.*

She took her time
And then she took mine
But it don't bother me
No, it don't bother me

She gave me a nickel
She said it was a dime
But it don't bother me
No, it don't bother me

And I ain't lyin', I'll just go on tryin'
These are better days than yesterday

Why do I bother looking for trouble?
Trouble will always find me
I'll figure it out one way or the other
I'm not gonna let it bother me

She took my life
She took her sweet time
As far as I can see
As far as the eye can see

In the eye of the beholder
It's so much colder
As far as the eye can see
As far as I can see

Where I once had a vision
It's just endless indecision
These are troubled waters we've survived before
So many times before
So many times before

Why do I bother looking for trouble?
Trouble will always find me
I'll figure it out one way or the other
I'm not gonna let it bother me

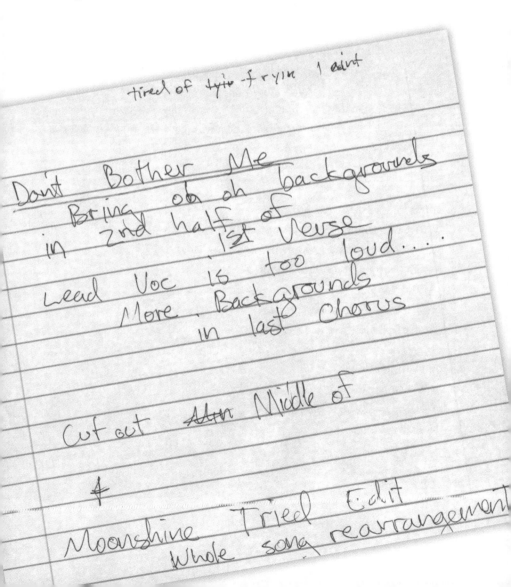

"MORGAN'S DOG"

Soul Asylum was asked to make a Christmas song for a record to benefit teens in need. I've always been very cynical about writing Christmas songs, but I accepted the challenge because I thought the cause was good. I also saw it as an opportunity for me to address the gun problem in America. However, it wasn't what the people who were making the benefit record were looking for, and "Morgan's Dog" was not included on the Christmas album.

Around this time, Morgan Spurlock was producing a documentary series for CNN called Inside Man. *I love documentaries and proper investigative reporting, and I think Morgan Spurlock is brilliant. In one of the first episodes, he shows how easy it is to get a gun in America. He starts out talking about how his dad gave him a gun when he was a kid, and he shot his own dog by accident—I may have embellished that or mixed it up to make it work for the song. It's like a beautiful and disturbing proverb for me: Give your kid a gun for Christmas, and he shoots the dog, and now he understands why guns are not cool. I thought it was hilarious as a premise for a Christmas song, and it had a message.*

It was an icy Christmas morning
When a boy named Morgan shot his dog that day
Man, he loved that dog, and boy, he loved that gun
When he found it underneath the tree that day

Raised his gun for the first time
Took careful aim at the bull's-eye

But shot his dog instead
Now Morgan's dog is dead
And the .22's his new best friend
Now that Morgan's dog is dead

Now the new .22 is always close at hand
Now he's hunting for a new best friend
He can't get it out, out of his head
He said, "I will never miss that shot again"

With one hand on the Bible
The other eye on survival

But now Morgan's dog is dead
He shot his own dog dead
And a .22's his new best friend
Now that Morgan's dog is dead

You got to get a gun just in case you're attacked
Sure hope you don't have an accident
And shoot someone that you probably shouldn't have
Oh no, you should never, ever get a gun

You'll probably shoot your own damn dog
And your dog would be dead
Can't get it through your head
Home and head to bed

Morgan's dog is dead
Yes, Morgan's dog is dead
After all is done and said
Morgan's dog's still dead

"CHANGE OF FORTUNE"

I probably worked on the song "Change of Fortune" for about eight years. I'm still not sure I got it right, but I gave it my best shot. Winston Roye, the bass player, said something like, "Fuck this, let's put the record out, and let's call it Change of Fortune." I said fine, because we gotta call it something.

This song was pivotal for me. I was trying to tie New Orleans rhythms into what I was doing with my music. Lyrically, the song is hopeful that things will change for the better, which I'm sure everyone hopes for.

What is the matter with me?
It's always raining or snowing
It's stuck inside me somewhere
I don't know where I'm going

What about the time
What about the drinks
What about the way
The way that we think
Now I'm getting nowhere
I could get to know you, c'mon

Change, change of fortune
Right, right on time
If you got the fruit
I got the orchard
All the times I tortured you
I could change your fortune too

What is the meaning of this insensitive violence?
What is it that you're asking?
Is it nothing but silence?

What about the time
What about the kids
What about the things
The things that we did
Now I'm getting nowhere
I could get to know you, c'mon

Change, change of fortune
Right, right on time
If you got the fruit
I've got the orchard
All the times I tortured you
I could change your fortune too

What is the meaning of this?
This ain't getting us nowhere

Change, change of fortune
Right, right on time
If you got the fruit
I've got the orchard
All the times I tortured you
I could change your fortune too

"COOL"

*"Cool" reflects another approach to rhythm that would not have happened
had I not lived in New Orleans for seventeen years. If you're from a place like
Minneapolis and then you spend time in New York or Los Angeles, it seems
like everybody thinks they're so fucking cool. When I got to New Orleans, I
noticed these older guys who were just cool by nature. They'd been playing
music forever, and they're cool because they can play. They're just gifted
musicians who have nice suits on, and they look pretty cool. I wasn't a New
Orleans dandy who could play the fuck out of an instrument. It inspired me
to decide that I needed to either get better or quit.*

You could be my guardian angel
Won't be calling, dial a stranger
Day by day, night by night
Let me know that you're all right

Tell me now am I cool enough
Cool enough for you?
What do I got to do to be
Cool enough to hang with you?

I'll just sit and keep to myself
Just assume I'll be someone else
I'll be there when you start to cry
You won't wish I'm some other guy

Tell me now am I cool enough
Cool enough for you?
What do I got to do to be
Cool enough to hang with you?

You could show me all the angles

Tell me now am I cool enough
Cool enough for you?
What do I got to do to be
Cool enough to hang with you?

9-8-2014

Moonshine
Change of Fortune
Catching Fire
Cool 09
Dealing 09
Dont Bother Me
Can't Help It
Doomsday
Ladies Man
Make it real
Morgans Dog
Oh Karl
Super Sonic
Common Man

soul asylum

Hurry Up and Wait

Hurry Up and Wait is scheduled for release a few months from now, as I'm putting the finishing touches on this book. I was doing the dishes recently and the thought popped into my head, "Shit, I have a book *and* a record coming out. Life could be worse." This is a first for me, and it's pretty cool, I guess. It's also a little strange that the lyrics for these songs will appear in a book before the record comes out. Trust me, they're better with music. The music is a little on the tender side—which means I'll probably make the next record really hard.

Currently, I'm feeling pretty positive. We just played a sold-out show at First Avenue and received a lot of encouraging feedback. But I'm keeping my expectations realistic, considering that people don't buy records the way they used to.

Hurry Up and Wait was probably half written in New Orleans and half written in Minneapolis. It spans the failure of my marriage and the beginning of not being able to see my kid. This record has a pretty raw and honest batch of tunes.

As for the record's title, I've heard lots of musicians talk about how being in a band is a lot of fucking waiting. You travel and travel and travel, and then you play for ninety minutes, and then you travel and travel and travel some more. You're always scrambling to get from one place to another, and then you're sitting around waiting for a plane or waiting for the show to start—it's endless. I wrote the expression "hurry up and wait" on a piece of paper along with other possible album titles, and this one stood out to me. It feels accurate in describing what it's like to be in a band.

"THE BEGINNING"

"The Beginning" is written with the sentiment of "you never know unless you try," and figuring out how to integrate one's self into a social situation. There's a lot of starting over in life, and I'm trying to look at the future with a bright, shiny attitude.

Everyone's waiting to see if you're coming
Outta your shell for a while
Cupid and Casper were asking about ya
You used to be so wild

I know how it is, you get drunk at a party
It seems there's someone you should call
Then the cycle begins; you decide to stay in
You don't talk to anyone at all

Never know what you might find
You never know what you leave behind

This is the beginning of a great adventure
Now's not the time to step aside

I've had my share of missteps and delusions
Head trips and tales that are tall
Every conclusion is better than never
Happily after all

You dig yourself out of the tangled-up barbed wire
Fightin' over every wall
And then you get over; you pull yourself up
You pull yourself up by the straps of your overalls

Never know what you might find

You never know what you leave behind
This is the beginning of a great adventure
Leavin' with you

This is the beginning of a great adventure
Now's not the time to leave it behind

I'm right behind you
Behind you all the way
And when I find you
We'll be on our way

Everyone's waiting to see if you're coming
Out of your shell for a while
Cupid and Casper were asking about you
You used to be so wild

And this is the beginning of a great adventure
Now's not the time to step aside

This is the beginning of a great adventure
Now's not the time to leave it behind

Leavin' with you

"IF I TOLD YOU"

I've had friends from New Orleans ask me if the sun ever comes out in Minnesota during the winter. If you were born in Minneapolis, maybe you just get used to it being gray a lot. But you can see how much it eats away at people from sunnier climates. You can really start to miss the sun. You get cabin fever and feel depressed.

My son lives in New Orleans, whereas I mostly live in Minneapolis these days, and I miss seeing him. On my records, I've always tried to resist anything that resembles a traditional "love song." In "If I Told You," what I love the most is my kid; I've never missed anyone like that.

This song is also talking about the fear of trusting your feelings and trying to be comfortable with someone else. Then, when it doesn't work out, you question why you ever thought it would.

If I asked for forgiveness,
Does it mean that I did it?
Is it really that bad; am I that hard to live with?

If I told you I loved you,
Would you hold it against me?

I've seen every shade of gray
I can't wait another day
For summer to come

I miss the sun
It's something that I try to overcome

If I walked to the corner,
Would you put up a red light?
Would you hold it against me if it didn't turn out right?

Please don't make me say it
I would never regret it
If I told you I loved you, would you let me forget it?

I've seen every shade of gray
The clouds just seem to come my way
Come rain or come shine

I miss the sun
Every day is someday will come
Don't you know that I miss the sun?
Lie and wait for summer to come

I know that you're busy
Don't hold it against me
If I told you I loved you, would you hold it against me?

I miss the sun
Every day is someday will come
Don't you know that I miss the sun?
I miss my son

If I told you I loved you,
Would you hold it against me?

"GOT IT PRETTY GOOD"

In "Got It Pretty Good," I'm not really talking about my personal state of well-being. It's more about having an instinct for figuring out what's wrong with someone or what's right with someone; either you've got that instinct, or you don't.

It's also about obsession, in a way, when you have this feeling of helplessness that you can't do anything about, and that isn't necessarily a bad feeling. It's the way I feel about music. I caught the bug, and now I have an itch to do it that I can't get rid of. It's hard to explain, but it's a good feeling.

Well, I went to the doctor, I was feelin' bad
I went to church trying to see what they had
The psychiatrist sent me back to the priest
He just said, "keep your trousers creased"
You know I got it
I got it pretty good

I tried being mean
I tried being nice
I tried taking all of your advice

It's time to shine
A fine time to remind me
Well, I'm just fine
A fine time to unwind
And now's your time to shine

I got it pretty good

I got the joke, I'm on my knees
I tried bein' nice, I tried bein' mean
Livin' my life just keepin' it clean
I got the fever
I got it pretty good

I need a good hammer
And a couple of nails
Build me a boat
I'm gonna set my sails

My time to shine
It's a fine time to remind me
I'm doing just fine
If I could find the time
Now's your time to shine

It ain't good or bad, it ain't wrong or right
I ain't giving up; gonna stay in the fight
I'm unraveling, I'm gonna unwind
I'm winding down if I could find the time
I got it
I got it pretty good

I tried being mean
I tried being nice
I tried taking all of your advice

It's time to shine
A fine time to remind me
To live your life
Like it's on the line
And now's your time to shine

I got it pretty good

"MAKE HER LAUGH"

I wrote "Make Her Laugh" when my marriage was coming to an end. There's nothing more satisfying to me than making someone laugh, even if that someone doesn't seem to like me very much. That little bit of feedback, a laugh, is meaningful. I tend to make a joke out of everything, though. It keeps me from boring myself to death.

Up the river without a raft
You've done your worst with your better half
You better think of something fast
You better make her laugh

Well, it's after hours at the break of dawn
You've made your bed all day long
I must be doing something wrong
Are those tears of joy, or are you just cryin'?

Just when you think you've had enough
And you're tired of tryin' to suck it up
I know you can make her laugh
Like a child on a carnival ride
Laugh the mascara right off her eyes
As she's walkin' away, just give it one more try
I know you can make her laugh

Well, you can leave when you want
But please leave us laughing
Leave us wondering what the fuck just happened
Your ironic cynical sarcastic sense of humor's
Got me wondering, if I ever had a chance

You know you can't make her love you
But you sure can make her cry
You can't make her make up her mind
Just when you think you've had enough
And you're tired of tryin' to suck it up
I know you can make her laugh
Like a child on a carnival ride
Laugh the mascara right off her eyes
As she's walkin' away, give it one more try
I know you can make her laugh

I'm bombin' tonight
Crickets fill the sky
I'm dyin' on the vine
When I see you smile again
Well, I can make her laugh

Now I'm first in line for the last word now
None of the sadness or madness has yet to die down
There's nothing left to do but laugh out loud
It was all just a joke anyhow

So make her laugh
Like a child on a carnival ride
Laugh the mascara right off her eyes
As she's walking away, just give it one more try
I know you can make her laugh

Make her laugh

I know you can make her laugh

"BUSY SIGNALS"

"Busy Signals" involves technology and the utter frustration of trying to keep up with it. It's strange for me to think about how many younger people there are who never knew a life where everyone didn't carry a phone around. I guess I kind of miss the days when people were focused on what is happening beyond the tiny screen in front of their faces. Life is passing them by.

Please relieve me
Leave before someone sees me
The cloak outlasts the dagger
What a mystery
I don't know who done it, I just know it ain't me

You know that you want to
You know that I want to
You know that you—

What's wrong with this telephone?
This telephone used to work fine
Beats someone's telephone
Some telephone better than mine
What's wrong with this telephone?
What's wrong with this?

She's so easy
Her signals always busy
She holds the rights to women
Exclusively
She's the one that you'll never be

You know that you want to
You know that I want to
You know that you—

What's wrong with this telephone?
This telephone used to work fine
What's wrong with this telephone?
This telephone's better than mine
What's wrong with this telephone?
What's wrong with this?

Please go easy
Please go easy on me
The ocean tracks a river
Deliver me
To a place where I belong

You know that you want to
You know that I want to
You know that you—

What's wrong with this internet?
This internet used to work fine
What's wrong with this picture?
This picture used to be mine
What's wrong with this telephone?
What's wrong with this?

"SOCIAL BUTTERFLY"

I suppose I've felt a little lost since I left New Orleans. I've had to put a lot of faith into finding company among strangers. Getting out there and meeting people isn't always the easiest thing to do, but it's a big part of what I do. I guess I'm still trying to find my place in this world.

When I was younger
I thought I would die
Now I'm a little bit older
I still go out at night

I need someone to talk to
Hope I say something right
I go home alone
A social butterfly

I'm gonna come outta my coma
Gonna try to make things right
Stay out all night, tryin' to get a bite
Like a social butterfly

Now I'm just like a moth
Flyin' into the fire
And I fly by night
Lookin' for the nearest light

I saw you at the party
And we got in a fight
And now I miss you like
Yellow to the color blind

And I'm comin' outta my coma
I'm gonna come out tonight
Lookin' for a little reaction
I'm like a social butterfly

If I could do
What I wanna do with you
I'd crawl right back
Into my cocoon

You know I'm gonna come outta my coma
I'm gonna set the night on fire
I'll see you there
Don't be square
You're a social butterfly
Like a social butterfly
A social butterfly

"DEAD LETTER"

I've heard tell of a dead letter office at the post office. I imagine piles of letters written to Santa Claus. But there are tons of other letters that never got to the intended recipient. So many thoughts and messages and sentiments are sitting there, lost and forgotten. People work their whole lives to express themselves, and sometimes it just goes nowhere.

"Dead Letter" is contemplative and certainly not a party anthem. It's the message of the unheard people, the voices that fall on deaf ears.

Dead letter, dead letter
Of immaculate intention
It's written in blood that flows through the pen tip
Dead letter, dead letter
Never to deliver
The message of love I wanted to give her

Well, she sent a dead letter
To the book on the shelf
She'd revealed some secrets
She didn't want to tell
She died on the day that her baby was born
And the dead letter rests in the used bookstore

Dead letter, dead letter
Addressed straight to hell
It's written to someone; it's written quite well
Dead letter, dead letter
Will never be read
I'll write you a letter, as long as it's dead

There was no response
And they thought they had lost him
To drugging and drinking cough syrup
When they caught up with him
He just sat on the floor
In a pile of dead letters he just couldn't finish

Dead letter, dead letter
Addressed to you
It says that I'm sorry, explains the whole truth
I sent it to you so long ago
I thought that you got it, I just didn't know

"LANDMINES"

We know forgotten landmines are a problem. We can imagine how tragic it is to come across a landmine that has been left behind. A forgotten landline can also bring a kind of disaster—although certainly not nearly as disastrous as being blown to bits. The only people who call me on my landline are politicians or people trying to get money or scare me into some sort of fraud. It does make one approach the area with trepidation. If I stop answering my landline, it's as if I'm deciding not to enter that field of emotional landmines.

Landmines and landlines are both relics that can still be reactivated, usually for all the wrong reasons.

Well, call me on my landline
I ain't gonna answer
I can't talk to robots
I can't take those chances
A landline's better than a landmine
I guess I'll take my chances

You'll find the bodies buried
Right on down the road
Right between the landmines
Ready to explode
Landlords and lawyers on the front line
Stompin' on those landmines

So watch where you walk
Tread light
You better watch your step
One step at a time
When you're walkin' through that field of landmines

Your papa was a preacher
Your mama was a dancer
You never know
They're pretty old
They might have the answer
Left a slice out last night
Might be right where the ants were

Eggshells and earthquakes
Crackin' underfoot
You never know
When she might blow
The devil's on the loose
The telephone is ringin'
I don't need bad news

So watch where you walk
Tread light
You better watch your step
One step at a time
When you're walkin' through a field of landmines

Well, a landline's better than a landmine
This much I know
So call me on my landline
I don't have a phone
A landline's better than a landmine
That's one thing fo' sho

So watch where you walk
Tread light
Watch your step
One step at a time
You're walkin' through a field of landmines

"HERE WE GO"

When you're on the road or on tour, it's always, "the show must go on." It can be downright daunting at times. You have to throw your stuff in a bag to catch a plane or get your gear on stage for the show and make it work. It's not always easy.

Here we go
Where we're going I don't know
Like an unholy ghost
Flyin' much too low

I'll follow you down to hell my friend
No matter where you go
I've followed every word that you said
No matter where you go

I wish I was somewhere
I wish I was anywhere
If I could be anywhere
I'd wish I were with you

Well, here we go
A shovel plowin' through the snow
Takin' it blow by blow
Is this some kind of joke?

I'll fall for you when you fall through the cracks
No matter where you go
I'll track you down; I'll follow your tracks
No matter where you go

I wish I was somewhere
I wish I was anywhere
If I could be anywhere
I wish I were with you

Here we go
Carrying on with the show
And what I miss the most
We're heading for the coast

You know I wish I was somewhere
I wish I was anywhere
Now that you're gone
I wish I were with you

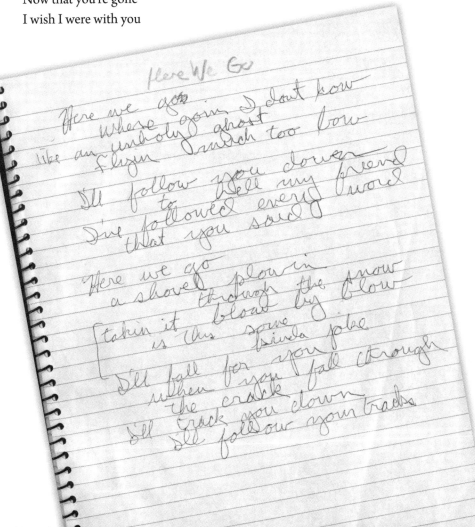

"FREEZER BURN"

In "Freezer Burn," I'm talking about people turning out to be not who you thought they were. Some people turn out to be cooler than you thought; some people are just crazy. But there's a surprise under every shirt. Generally, I think people are good inside, but what we find never ceases to amaze me.

Please return my bleeding heart
For it suffers freezer burn
Please take it out to thaw
I still got so much to learn

I need a rope, need a joke, need a rope
Ain't gonna tie me down
Loosen up, loosen up, I'm losin' hope
I think I'm losing ground

You really made a believer outta me
All the signs say if you can't stand it you should set it free
I never thought you'd turn out who you turned out to be
You really made a believer out of me

If you wanna take my hand
Or you've got a better plan
I've come to lead you all astray
I've still got so much to say

So load 'em up, loadin' up your weapons
Sharpen up your pen
Put it on, put your thinking cap on
I think we're goin' in

You really made a believer outta me
All the signs say if you can't stand it you should set it free
I never thought you'd turn out who you turned out to be
You really made a believer out of me

Cold ice water falls from the buildings above
Wheels turn and grind the gears of love
If everything goes right it ends up in its place
You really made a believer outta me
I never thought you'd turn out who you turned out to be
You really made a believer

Freezer Burn
You Know you made a believer outta me
and i'll believe as far as the eye can see
I was never much one for
the fortune tellers

"SILENT TREATMENT"

I don't believe in stonewalling as a strategy when it comes to relationships, but sometimes you just have to shut your mouth and let the other person dig their own hole. We're led to believe that people from Minnesota have passive-aggressive tendencies. I've definitely been in relationships where both parties decided that it's easier to not even try to communicate. It's incredibly sad when that happens.

Also, the quietness of a snowy night in Minneapolis is evoked in "Silent Treatment," like I did in "Never Really Been." In this case, it's an apocalyptic scenario in which all the people are gone. The raindrops are full of bile and toxic waste, and there's no one left.

When the silent treatment gets so loud it's buzzing in my head
Your lips are moving, tells I should be somewhere else instead
Take a chance on today

She said she was a mermaid
She said she liked horses

Then the silence finally breaks
You took all you could take
There's no one there

So you try to minimize it
Then you try to compromise it
No one really cares

The city streets are filled with sheets of raindrops filled with bile
The silence is so deafening it somehow makes me smile
Take a chance on tonight

She said she was a mermaid
She said she liked horses
She said she loved unicorns
I'd never bet on the dragon

When the silence finally breaks
You took all you could take
No one cares

Still you try to minimize it
Then you try to compromise it
No one's really there

When the ice melts off the lake and it reflects on what is fake
And you're skating somewhere, swimming I was losing every race
One stolen moment might turn out right

She said she was a mermaid
She said she liked horses
Never bet on the unicorn
Never bet on the dragon

When the silence finally breaks
You find out just what's fake
There's no one there

So you try to minimize it
Then you try to compromise it
No one really cares

"HOPPED UP FEELIN'"

"Hopped Up Feelin'" is an attempt to turn things around and write a song about feeling good. A hopped-up feelin' is a good feeling—let's jump up and down and have fun; let's leave our troubles in the dust and stop whining.

It may seem like there's a drug reference in the song, but not really. I mean, there's nothing better than feeling love. Unfortunately, people often don't feel it or don't get enough of it, and they turn to whatever they can find to make themselves feel better. But there isn't really any substitute, and you can end up going down a slippery slope in a bad direction. You want to feel that high, and if you can't get it from your loved ones, you go someplace else. And all too often that place is chemical dependency. To be able to depend on love is a beautiful thing. You gotta depend on something. But drugs are definitely not the answer.

Don't you ever wanna leave me alone?
Don't you ever wanna watch my back?
Can't you ever even leave it alone?
You don't ever wanna walk my path

You never see me when I'm keeping it together
You only see me when I'm falling apart
Got a feeling, a hopped-up feeling
It ain't worth stealin' 'cause I'm givin' it away to everyone

Are you ever gonna leave it at home?
Would you ever make me swallow my pride?
Would you ever try to spit me out?
Would you ever stop and wonder why?

I could see it if we never got together
I would never find my place in the sun
Got a feeling, a hopped-up feeling
It ain't worth stealin' 'cause I'm givin' it away to everyone
Drugs are a substitute for love
And love is a substitute for nothing at all

Nothing's going to come between us now
Nothing's going to make me change my mind
If I never ever see you again
Nothing's ever going to take away my good time

You never see me when I'm keeping it together
You only see me when I'm falling apart
Got a feeling, a hopped-up feeling
It ain't worth stealin' 'cause I'm givin' it away to everyone

Got a feeling, a hopped-up feeling

"SILLY THINGS"

If I had listened to the better side of some of the advice I've been given, I never would have joined a band or formed a band or gone down this path. I often think it was a bad move. I've done a lot of things that I don't necessarily regret, but you know, you have to try everything. My approach has always been to proceed with reckless abandon and just go for it. And you know, I'm still trying to figure it out.

I've done a lot of silly things
I've found out just what trouble brings
You used to wear my silly ring
While I listened to my ears ring
I've done a lot of silly things

I used to think that I was cool
Break each and every single rule
Now all the rules are just the same
It's just a silly game
I used to do a lot of things

And when I fail, I will fail without you
And my mistakes I'll always answer to
And if I cared anymore
To see it like the truth
I've done a lot of silly things
And I know just what trouble brings
I've done a lot of silly things

I used to like the way you walk
You used to like the way I talk
I used to do a lot of things
I used to think that I could sing
I've done a lot of silly things

You used to like the way I moved
You used to think that I was smooth
And if I ever had a chance
I would ask you out again
I've done a lot of stupid things

And when I fail, I will fail without you
I've been let down so many times
No one to blame but myself
To keep from getting down
I've done a lot of stupid things
And I know just what trouble brings
I've done a lot of silly things

I've done a lot of silly things
Now I know just what trouble brings
You used to wear my silly ring
I've done a lot of stupid things
I've done a lot of silly things

But when I play, I will play without you
It's every man and woman for themselves
I feel I've learned the hard way
To put you before myself

I've done a lot of silly things
I've done a lot of stupid shit
I'm still tryin' to deal with it

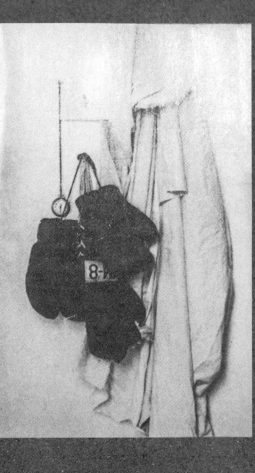

Twin/Tone RECORDS

TTR 8677C

SOUL ASYLUM
TIME'S INCINERATOR

20 UNRELEASED CUTS FROM PUBERTY TO LATENT
ADOLESCENCE – LOUD FAST RULES CUM SOUL
ASYLUM EXPOSE THEIR UGLY PAST, 1981-1986

TWIN/TONE RECORDS, 445 OLIVER AVENUE SOUTH, MINNEAPOLIS, MN 55405

BONUS TRACKS & LEFTOVERS

I t sounds corny, but to a songwriter, their songs are like children. The struggle is to get the stork to land the song on a record so people can hear it. These are the ones that got away. There are many more.

"STRAIGHT UP"

"Straight Up" was written around the same time as Grave Dancers Union. *During this period I was heavy into acoustic music. This song seemed to sum up a lot of my feelings about what's real and what is kind of bullshit. I always hoped it would end up on a record, but here are the lyrics.*

You know the galaxy's full of black holes
We don't know which ones have the pay tolls
Take a look out; I'll take a look inside

This is a whole new kind of illusion
Based on a brand-new kind of confusion
Built on wise decisions based on foolish pride

And you wonder why you wasted all this time
Trying to find gold in a salt mine
And now you've reached the limit
But the limit is the sky
Straight up one more
Straight up one more time
This is a character assassination

This is a character that needs a vacation
Too soon too long too much for one mind
You gotta step back and take inventory
You're only seeing one side of the story
And a good story is changing all the time

There is always one more sucker doing fine
One more trucker driving that white line
Delivering nothing, to no one everywhere

Straight up one more
Straight up one more time

It's much too easy to give up
It's much too hard to get up
To another day just like yesterday

And this time there is no escape this time
And any explanation would be fine
And now you've reached the limit
But the limit is the sky

Straight up one more
Straight up one more time

"CAN'T EVEN TELL"

"Can't Even Tell" is a song about wondering what the fuck is going on, both internally and externally. I was trying to assimilate to a world where I just didn't fit in. It was an outtake from Let Your Dim Light Shine *and became a single from the soundtrack for* Clerks, *which was Kevin Smith's first movie. I think people know the song thanks to the movie.*

I may never get what I want
But I'm happy to just die trying
And I hope I ain't done nobody wrong
But I miss you smiling

And I'm looking for a cure 'cause I'm bored to tears
And I'm stuck in here, stuck out here, stuck in here

We lived through another day
It's a good excuse to celebrate
Take a number, knock on wood
We'll find a reason to feel good

I know you know I want to know how I feel
I can't even tell

No one knows nothing about me
I'm happy just to keep 'em guessing
No one sees what I see
This is my blessing

And I'm looking for a way to get out of here
Get me out of here

We lived through another day
It's a good excuse to celebrate
Take a number, knock on wood
We'll find a reason to feel good

I know you know you wanna know how I feel
I can't even tell

I'm out of here
I know you know I want to know how I feel
I can't tell

I know you know I'll tell you if it's real
It's subtle as a bell
I can't even tell

"DIE IN YOUR ARMS"

What can I say? Sometimes a man falls for a woman.

Dad must have been drinking the night I was conceived
A flailing, lost, delirious sperm
A semen lost at sea
But someway, somehow I found you
And the journey has been long
A troubled, songless singer who had finally found a song
And I don't wanna do you no harm
I just wanna die in your arms

The bitter, biting cold froze the waves within their tracks
Trapped beneath the ice never to come back
The skaters whirled and twirled and glided, effortless in motion
Laughing in their blissful dance upon the frozen ocean

Am I the only one that this happens to?
Does this mother know no other?
Well, my mother taught me enough about love to know you are my lover

The ice cracked and crackled
And from it steam would rise
Her wings spread far and wide and whisked away the sky
And though I cannot see her now, I still look everyplace
Washed upon the shore, saved by your humbling grace
And I don't wanna do you no harm
I just wanna die in your arms

"LUCKY ONE"

I was temporarily living in a house in Baltimore at the time I wrote "Lucky One." The house had really good acoustics. I was just singing random things, and this song came out. I always remember the reverb produced in that weird, old house when I think back on this song. This was an outtake from Candy from a Stranger.

Hold me in my time
One day I'll be gone
And you'll see me as a thing that happened long, long ago

Think I thought too much
Reaching out of touch
But I'll know you when I see you coming
Toss away my crutch

Take your reactions as coming attractions
From dust that you keep on the shelf

Sometimes I feel like I lost my life, lost my life

Running low on luck
Nowhere to go but up
But I'll know everything is all right when I see you again

Sprung from the cages
You crawl from the pages
Of tales that nobody tells

Sometimes I feel like I'm so alone, there's no one home, all alone

Shelter me from hate
Don't make me a visitor
And you'll see me as a thing that happens each and every day
Good things are coming
And from it, you're running
They'll catch up to you someday

Sometimes I feel like the lucky one

"LONELY FOR YOU"

"Lonely for You" was written sometime between moving to New Orleans and making Candy from a Stranger *in Miami. I had become so alienated at this point in my life. My relationships with cab drivers were some of my best conversations. The desire to feel comfortable was insatiable. I was all over the country all the time. It's strange being lonely in public.*

Barefoot and pregnant she tries not to bend
The ear of the doctor's not much of a friend
The doctor's on location missing his kids
And wondering where she went to live

Spend time alone and look after your life
Remember your loved ones, your boyfriends, your wives
And if you are lonely and she's lonely, too
She will stay lonely for you

Come what may
Come some day
She will stay lonely for you

Patiently waiting for taxies to come
To take you away from all you have become
The driver tells stories like he's your best friend
And you hope the ride never ends

To all of the ones who have got no one else
Who keep their own time and look after themselves
Someday you'll meet someone lonely as you
And he will stay lonely for you

Come what may
Come some day
And I will stay lonely for you

"LOSIN' IT"

At the time, it seemed a lot of people were just complaining about the most superficial things. My reaction to other people telling me how difficult their life is, is to keep my mouth shut and listen. So, I'm going a little bit crazy at this point—losing it. I wanted someone to acknowledge that I'm also having a hard time. I don't know: life is frustrating. Get over it.

This song first appeared on an untitled promo EP for Candy *from a* Stranger. *It was also included in the Japanese release for that album, but not the original US release.*

Go ahead
Spit it out
I can take it
Don't do this
Don't do that
Try and fake it
I have seen it all

Tell me there's
Something wrong
Make me see it
How I try
I must be wrong
It must be me
I've been wrong before

And I confess
That I am having a hard time
I confess
That your hard time's harder than mine

When it's over, I'm coming over
Use your shoulder; it'll soon be over
I'm losin' it!

Suck it up
Rip it out
Still I'm learnin'
Light it up
Put it out
Keep it burnin'
I've been burned before

Come on out
I know you can
Make me happy
Little smile
Just a hand
Make it happen
I have smiled before

I confess
That I am having a hard time
And I confess
That your hard time's harder than mine

When it's over, I'm coming over
Use your shoulder; it'll soon be over

But I'm losin' it!

I am having a hard time

"CANDY FROM A STRANGER"

"Candy from a Stranger" is sort of like a deal with a devil. It goes back to my fears of creeps on the street abducting children, or selling bad drugs, or whatever the case may be. I find it kind of funny: you got a guy thinking about killing himself, and then someone offers to do it for him. Then you have the old man dealing with mortality whose doctors enter the realm of material exchange for a longer life.

As things go, this was the title track for Candy from a Stranger, *but it was left off the record.*

Well, a young boy wants to die
Thinking he might try taking his own life
Then up from behind
With a gun in his side, they said:

Give me all your money
Your money or your life
Candy from a stranger

Candy from a stranger

Well, an old man said he wants to live
Telling the doctor he's got more left to give
Doctors says that you pay or you die

Give me all your money
Your money or your life
Candy from a stranger

Candy from a stranger

Give me all your money
Your money or your life
Candy from a stranger

"ONE WAY CONVERSATION"

I often refer to a world where everyone talks and no one listens. It seems to be one of those afflictions called reality. I don't know, what do you think?

"One Way Conversation" was an outtake from And the Horse They Rode in On.

If I were you I'd get away
Nothing nice left to say
So tie your shoes
Pull up your pants
Pull yourself out of that trance

'Cause I'm tired of fantasy
Want something I can touch
Something I can see
Are you there?
Can you still feel?
Is this a joke?
Does this seem real?
Or just a cheap, cheap dream
For those who sleep?

The chosen ride
The desperate walk
Doers do
And you just talk
And when you speak to me
It's like a one-way conversation
Useless information
Get me a translator

Take a look
A look and see
What your life has come to be
It wanders on
It is not lost
It's just a coin
You've got to toss
Into your deep blue sea

Of all your one-way conversations
Cross communication
Get an operator
Get me anyone

Bold system of living
Talking without listening
Taking without giving

It's cynical
It's not quite young
Now mama's boy
Has got a son
Faster yet
And smarter still
With father's guns
And mother's pills
It's just a cheap, cheap dream

One-way conversation
Not my imagination
I know you're in there somewhere

TIME'S INCINERATOR

T ime's Incinerator is a collection that was released on cassette only, and it still can only be found in that format. It's various recordings the band had done in different low-budget situations, and a few things that slipped through the cracks on previous releases. There is also some live stuff on there. There are a couple of songs from my high school band, the Schitz, and some that I had written more recently. Our sense of humor is reflected in a lot of the songs on Time's Incinerator.

The cassette documents the very first time we went into the studio as a band. We met a guy named Bob Caine, who had a studio in a church, and the magic ensued. We had no idea what we were doing, and the memory of it is probably more romantic than the actual experience. But it was a good way to start off as a band.

Time's Incinerator includes some of our favorite cover songs from the day, too. They're listed in the discography at the back of this book, and they offer a sense of the type of music we were experimenting with at the time.

The jacket of the cassette tape really describes it best: "20 unreleased cuts from puberty to latent adolescence—Loud Fast Rules cum Soul Asylum expose their ugly past, 1981–1986."

"DRAGGIN' ME DOWN"

"Draggin' Me Down" is a punk rock/blues song. It's filled with frustration and trying to get it out. I'm just trying to make something out of all the confusion, frustration, and anger of being young and directionless.

The pain keeps draggin' me down
Gonna rip it from my heart
Drown and shut out the sound
Comedy's about to start
The world's been draggin' me down
Prepare your inner child
I keep draggin' me down
Learned to run before I walked

It's only water, it's only rain, it's only teardrops, only pain
But it's draggin' me down, draggin' me down, draggin' me down

My mind keeps draggin' me down
Every time I stop to think
Time keeps pushing me down
The bodies are startin' to stink
The world keeps draggin' me down
Don't die, I wanna help
I keep draggin' me down
Can't even help myself

It's only water, it's only rain, it's only teardrops, it's only pain
But it's draggin' me down, draggin' me down, draggin' me down

C'mon make me smile
I'll be all right in a while
It's not like I have some special infection
I just want a little old-fashioned affection

Stop draggin' me down, draggin' me down, draggin' me down

It's only water, it's only rain, it's only teardrops, only pain
It's draggin' me down, draggin' me down, draggin' me down

its only water
its only rain
its only teardrops
its only pain

its only water
its only rain
i believe the poor boys
gone insane

look what youve done too yourself
my son - my boyfreind, nobody

"FREEWAY"

When I was a young innocent, I thought I would find a free way to live my life, but I basically ended up driving up and down a freeway instead.

I wanna see you in my rearview mirror
On down the freeway
Nobody said it would be easy

Freeway
Take me back to where I wanna be
And I can't change the time
And I can't change your mind
But I gotta find a freeway to run my way

Leeway, I need a little leeway
I've got to get some space surrounding me
Leeway, I need a little leeway
Make the best of nothin' left for me

And I can't find the time
Got to see what I can find
On down the freeway
To run my way

I'm not talkin'

Someday
I ain't waitin' around for someday
Someday
I'm gonna break away from all this someday

But I can't change your mind
And I can't change the time
But I gotta find a freeway to run my way

"THE SNAKE"

This song starts out, "Sssssssssssss . . ." The chorus is, "Ladies, don't fear the snake." I believe I'm talking about women not being afraid of men, but I can't decipher the words. It was a long time ago.

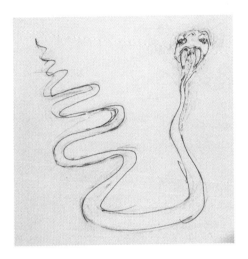

"JOB FOR ME"

"Job for Me" is pretty relatable, in that anyone who's a junior in high school is thinking about what he or she is going to do to make a living after they graduate.

Well, I want to find a job that's right for me
I just don't know what I wanna be
Well, I just don't know what I'm gonna do
I hope I don't ever have to work for you

Maybe I could be your bus driver
Maybe I could be your garbage man
Your garbage is what I deal with anyway
I'll try to keep on doing what I can

Well, I want to find a job that's right for me
I've run out of opportunities
Well, I just don't know what I wanna be
I hope I don't have to always work for free
A janitor or a politician
The only difference seems to be tuition
The Lone Ranger, that would be fun
Hand me my silver bullets and my gun

I want to find a job that's right for me
I've run out of opportunities
Give me some lifelong security
But you better be careful or you'll be workin' for me

Maybe I could be your doctor
Go to school and get my PhD
I wonder if I could ever make a living
Strummin' these old As, Gs, and Cs

"SWINGIN'"

"Swingin'" is about feelin' good about yourself.

Swingin'
I'm swingin'

Take it to the root one time, motherfuckers

"DO YOU KNOW"

When Loud Fast Rules was starting out, we would play a fascinating set of covers that included my, Danny's, and Karl's favorite songs. We were never going to be a cover band, but we needed to establish a musical base. And we still needed original material. "Do You Know" was one of the early original songs that I brought in. It was from my first band, the Schitz. It's the only song from my high school band that made it onto a Soul Asylum record. It's about learning to cope with stirring adolescent emotions.

Do you know what it's like to really hate somebody?
Or will you love me forever, 'cause you take all my funny money?
You got your plans all set, you're gonna be a big success
And you'd do anything to buy yourself respect

Cars and diamond rings, in houses, video things
And jewelry, London Fog
Big houses, little dogs

And do you know what it's like to really love somebody?
Or will you hate me forever, 'cause I'm not what you want me to be?
You got our little planet in the palm of your hand
You'd do anything to get your high-rise built on sand

Trips to far-away places, dollars, happy faces
Jewelry, London Fog
Pools and country clubs

What the fuck is wrong?
I can't just hate myself
I can't see right from wrong
My life's gone on too long

"SPACEHEAD"

There have been times in my life when I must have appeared to other people like I was out of it. Whether I was daydreaming or lost in thought, my mind was more open than most people's my age. Keeping an open mind is something that is very important to me. So, the space in my head is still under construction, and there are rooms available, even to this day.

So, you think I've got a problem?
So, you think it's all too clear?
Got a fucking mental disorder
Where's the fucking order around here?

I'm a spacehead, I'm not a stupid head
I am a spacehead, just open-minded

Spacehead

Why when I cry do I hang my head down low?
How do you move so fast but think so slow?
My favorite things I'll never know
Hang my head in the wind and let it blow

I'm a spacehead, I'm not a stupid head
Just open my head, I'm just a spacehead

Spacehead

Dancing in the library and the teacher says I'm a spacehead
Smoking in the church and the preacher says I'm a spacehead

The books are burning fast, the books are burning fast

I bet you know just what I'm saying
Maybe I am saying something else
The next decision that you make
Is probably gonna be a big mistake

I am a spacehead
Open up your head
I'm a spacehead
Just open-minded

Spacehead spacehead spacehead spacehead spacehead . . .

A SPACE HEADS
   MORE GUITARS
   WHAT IS DAN DOING?
B
C "SPACE HEAD !" missing
A
   ~~WEIRD~~ ~~SEA~~ BASS
   MORE BASS DRUM?

   RE-DO VOCS.
   TOO MUCH BASS
   VOCS. AT THE END
   Masqurade
   ~~the~~
   MORE GUIT + VOCS.
   MUSHY
SLOW   VOCS. PRTTY GOOD
       DANS LEADS ARE COOL
   TRY 2nd SAX TRACK
I def MORE DAN RYTHEM

II   VOCS. O.K. NOT GREAT
       PARTYS SAX COOL
       OUT SAX SQUACK
   SOLO A BIT BORING INTERESTING

III   VOCS. are abit lame
   BIGGER BOW !
   a little less high hat
   more crash
   END RE-MIX more more

"OUT OF STYLE"

*"Out of Style" was a pivotal song for me because it reflected how I was begin-
ning to realize that I could affect the world around me even with my limited
ability to make music at this time. I wrote this song when I was seventeen,
and things are hard to figure out at that age. Not only do you not know how
to look on the outside; you don't know what's going to happen to you on the
inside.*

*The people I was surrounded by in the punk rock scene were infatuated
by trends and fashion. People who weren't in the punk rock scene were even
worse.*

Don't you realize love's gone out of style?
Did you think that it would last for more than awhile?
Don't you forget to keep up with the fashion
This week's mannequins are not sporting passion

Oh, we must find something new
Oh, you hate me and I'll hate you

New boots and jacket, what else can I do?
I'm so in today, I'm stayin' away from you
Oh God, you bring me down, you're so out of style
Hand me down my walking stick and my fingernail file

Oh, we must find something new
Oh, run around and I'll piss on you

Can't you find a better way to waste all of your time?
Find someone to hate and join this special group of mine
I know what you're thinking, I know what you want to do
'Cause I'm a fashion connoisseur, and I've got my gun on you

"HEY BIRD"

I've always been fascinated by flying in helicopters. You really get a different view of things from up there. Anyway, I believe everyone at some time or other wonders what it would be like to be a bird. Being able to fly seems pretty fucking cool to me.

Hey now bird
I think I'd like to be like you
Flash a black silhouette
Across a sky so blue

Hey now bird
Do you laugh at me?
'Cause I do not see
All the things you see

I'm going to try to fly away

Well, I'm building a building
And smoke fills the air
Still you laugh and cry and sit and watch
You never cared

How do you get that feeling?
How do you get so high?
Do you run and jump and spread your wings and never die?

Fly away
I want to fly away

Hey now bird
Lying flat on the freeway
Will you sing one more song?
Will you never leave me?

"FRIENDS"

In the punk rock community in Minneapolis at the time, lots of kids were trying to get out of their parents' houses and were leaving home. I remember feeling like the people in the punk rock scene were my family. Friends had become very important to me, and I suppose the song "Friends" is a meditation on that.

I've been stressed by a dress stretched across the white cement
Can't identify the body, where it came, and where it went
And I see you walkin' on the street, and you look so all alone
I could be your mystery date, bring you candy, take me home

Don't you need someone to call?
Don't you need a friend to fall on?
I can't face myself alone
I need a real live friend

Well, I'm the toughest motherfucker that you ever did see
I never shed no tears in my life; I can hear you laugh at me
Well, I see you 'round the corner with your pants so goddamn tight
Do you think that all this money's gonna make everything all right?

Don't you need someone to call?
Don't you need a friend to fall on?
I can't face myself alone
I need a real live friend

I've got friends to take for granted, friends to talk behind my back
Friends who look you in the eye while they stab you in the back
I got friends to steal my girlfriend, friends that take you for a ride
Friends that make me hot, and friends who keep me cold inside
I got friends who sell me guilty pleasure, and I know friends just like you
Friends who scare my friends away and tell me what to do
I got so many goddamn friends, friends that I don't even know
When I need my friends the most, where did they go?

Don't you need someone to call?
Don't you need a friend to fall on?
I can't face myself alone
I need a real live friend

"YOUR CLOCK"

Anyone who knows me knows that I have a hard time getting places on time. Time seems like a conspiracy, like someone designed clocks just to make me late. When I wrote "Your Clock," I was working two jobs and going to school.

Your clock runs your silly life
Your clock runs your fuckin' wife
Cut you off if you're not on time
I can't give it up for your clock

Got an appointment to have some fun
Got an appointment to fire a gun
Guns are fun for everyone
I'll never give it up for your clock

Your clock tells you when to wait
Your clock tells you when to hate
Don't stop to think or you'll be late
I've had quite enough of your clock

Four o'clock I'll fall in love
Your clock guides you from above
I just can't take this push and shove
I won't run around for your clock

Your clock makes me wonder why
Your clock tells you vicious lies
Like when to live and when to die
I'm gonna have to stomp on your clock

"MASQUERADE"

The first part of "Masquerade" is like classic American hardcore. The second part is really bad jazz. The song deals with phoniness and appearances and people pretending that they're someone other than who they truly are.

You are invited to my masquerade

The truth is gonna come spillin' out, when I shed the mask
We'll find out what it's all about, when I shed the mask
The castles will come falling down
Let's give the circus back their clowns

Don't dare scare me

Parties, parties all the time, when I shed the mask
I'm tired of wasting my precious time, when I shed the mask
This same old scene is getting old
Besides, my feet are getting' cold

Don't dare scare me

This life and times are scandalous, when I shed the mask
Just take a tip from tricky Dick, when I shed the mask
It's all about your fuckin' money
It's all about a little more

Don't dare scare me

I'm so glad we could get together
Thank you for supplying the fun
Well, we took this time out to enjoy ourselves
Now let's just fucking get it done

Well, we're talk, talk, talking and talk, talk, talk, talking
Then maybe we'll have a little fight

Hush, hush, hush
Now don't admit that the reason we're here is just to get fucked tonight

This masquerade is over

Personal invitations only

I got my makeup on
I got my hair all done
I bet you can't even guess who I am

Well, I thought you were my friend
But then the troubles began
And that old identity set in

Well, I see no end to this bullshit, so let's talk politics
Where it's parties, parties, parties all the time
We got big long cars, we got movie stars
We got the three B's: the bigots, the bombs, and barriers

This masquerade is over

I didn't invite no black, hippie, hardcore, rich, poor,
Catholic, Jews, red, white, bastard mothers, blues
So, if you think you're something special,
You know I certainly didn't invite you

You know these costume parties they're such a good time
But I think I'm gonna have to be headin' home
It's funny how these social events
They just make me want to be alone

This masquerade is over

It's all over

It's over

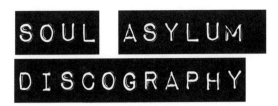

Say What You Will . . . Everything Can Happen

(original vinyl release)

RELEASED: AUGUST 24, 1984

Label: Twin/Tone

Producer: Bob Mould

"Long Day"

"Voodoo Doll"

"Money Talks"

"Stranger"

"Sick of That Song"

"Walking"

"Happy"

"Black and Blue"

"Religiavision"

Made to Be Broken

RELEASED: JANUARY 16, 1986

Label: Twin/Tone

Producer: Bob Mould

"Tied to the Tracks"

"Ship of Fools"

"Can't Go Back" (written by Dan Murphy)

"Another World, Another Day"

"Made to Be Broken"

"Never Really Been"

"Whoa!"

"New Feelings"

"Growing Pain"

"Lone Rider"
"Ain't That Tough"
"Don't It (Make Your Troubles Seem Small)"

Time's Incinerator
(cassette only)
RELEASED: JUNE 24, 1986
Label: Twin/Tone
Producer: Bob Mould and Soul Asylum
"Draggin' Me Down"
"Freeway"
"Broken Glass" (written by Dan Murphy)
"Goin' Down" (written by Micky Dolenz, Davy Jones, Peter Tork, Michael Nesmith, and Diane Hildebrand)
"The Snake"
"Hot Pants" (written by James Brown)
"Job for Me"
"Swingin'"
"Take It to the Root" (live)
"Fearless" (radio interview)
"Do You Know"
"Spacehead"
"Cocaine Blues" (written by T. J. Arnall and Johnny Cash)
"Out of Style"
"Nowhere to Go" (written by Dan Murphy)
"Hey Bird"
"Friends"
"Ramblin' Rose" (written by Marijohn Wilkin and Fred Burch)
"Your Clock"
"Masquerade"
"Soul Asylum" (written by Mecht Mensch)

While You Were Out
RELEASED: NOVEMBER 21, 1986
Label: Twin/Tone
Producer: Chris Osgood
"Freaks"
"Carry On"

"No Man's Land"

"Crashing Down" (written by Dan Murphy)

"The Judge"

"Sun Don't Shine"

"Closer to the Stars"

"Never Too Soon"

"Miracle Mile" (written by Dan Murphy)

"Lap of Luxury"

"Passing Sad Daydream"

Clam Dip and Other Delights

RELEASED: APRIL 14, 1988

Label: A&M

Producers: Soul Asylum and Tom Herbers

"Just Plain Evil"

"Chains" (written by the Wad)

"Secret No More"

"Artificial Heart"

"P-9"

"Take It to the Root"

Hang Time

RELEASED: APRIL 25, 1988

Label: A&M

Producers: Lenny Kaye and Ed Stasium

"Down on Up to Me"

"Little Too Clean"

"Sometime to Return"

"Cartoon" (written by Dan Murphy)

"Beggars and Choosers"

"Endless Farewell"

"Standing in the Doorway"

"Marionette"

"Ode"

"Jack of All Trades"

"Twiddly Dee"

"Heavy Rotation"

"Put the Bone In" (bonus track on CD release; written by Terry Jacks)

Say What You Will, Clarence . . . Karl Sold the Truck

(CD rerelease)

RELEASED: 1988

Label: Twin/Tone

Producer: Bob Mould

"Draggin' Me Down"

"Long Day"

"Money Talks"

"Voodoo Doll"

"Stranger"

"Do You Know"

"Sick of That Song"

"Religiavision"

"Spacehead"

"Walking"

"Broken Glass" (written by Dan Murphy)

"Masquerade"

"Happy"

"Black and Blue"

And the Horse They Rode in On

RELEASED: SEPTEMBER 4, 1990

Label: A&M

Producer: Steve Jordan

"Spinnin'"

"Bitter Pill"

"Veil of Tears"

"Nice Guys (Don't Get Paid)"

"Something Out of Nothing"

"Gullible's Travels" (written by Dan Murphy)

"Brand New Shine"

"Easy Street"

"Grounded"

"Be on Your Way"

"We 3"

"All the King's Friends"

Grave Dancers Union

RELEASED: OCTOBER 6, 1992
Label: Columbia
Producer: Michael Beinhorn
"Somebody to Shove"
"Black Gold"
"Runaway Train"
"Keep It Up"
"Homesick"
"Get on Out"
"New World"
"April Fool"
"Without a Trace"
"Growing into You"
"99%"
"The Sun Maid"

Let Your Dim Light Shine

RELEASED: JUNE 6, 1995
Label: Columbia
Producers: Butch Vig and Soul Asylum
"Misery"
"Shut Down"
"To My Own Devices"
"Hopes Up"
"Promises Broken" (written by Dan Murphy and Marc Perlman)
"Bittersweetheart"
"String of Pearls"
"Crawl" (written by Dave Pirner and Steve Jordan)
"Caged Rat"
"Eyes of a Child"
"Just Like Anyone"
"Tell Me When" (written by D. Pirner and L. Samuels)
"Nothing to Write Home About"
"I Did My Best"

Candy from a Stranger

RELEASED: MAY 12, 1998
Label: Columbia
Producer: Chris Kimsey
"Creatures of Habit"
"I Will Still Be Laughing"
"Close"
"See You Later"
"No Time for Waiting"
"Blood into Wine" (written by Dan Murphy and Elizabeth Herman)
"Lies of Hate" (written by Dave Pirner and Sterling Campbell)
"Draggin' the Lake"
"New York Blackout"
"The Game"
"Cradle Chain"
"Losin' It" (on the Japanese release)

Black Gold: The Best of Soul Asylum

(compilation album)
RELEASED: SEPTEMBER 26, 2000
Label: Columbia/Legacy

After the Flood: Live from the Grand Forks Prom

(live album)
Recorded: June 28, 1997
RELEASED: OCTOBER 5, 2004
Label: Columbia/Legacy
Producer: Jeff Magid
"School's Out" (written by Alice Cooper, et al.)
"Misery"
"Black Gold"
"See You Later"
"Without a Trace"
"Losin' It"
"Somebody to Shove"
"Just Like Anyone"
"The Tracks of My Tears" (written by Smokey Robinson, Pete Moore, and Marv
    Tarplin)

"Runaway Train"

"We 3"

"I Know" (written by Dionne Farris)

"Sexual Healing" (written by Marvin Gaye, Odell Brown, and David Ritz)

"The Game"

"I Can See Clearly Now" (written by Johnny Nash)

"Black Star"

"To Sir with Love" (written by Don Black and Mark London)

"Rhinestone Cowboy" (written by Larry Weiss)

Closer to the Stars: Best of the Twin/Tone Years

(compilation album)

RELEASED: APRIL 4, 2006

Label: Rykodisc

Producers: Bob Mould, Chris Osgood, Soul Asylum, Tom Herbers

The Silver Lining

RELEASED: JULY 11, 2006

Label: Legacy

Producers: John Fields and Steve Hodge

"Stand Up and Be Strong"

"Lately"

"Crazy Mixed Up World"

"All Is Well"

"Bus Named Desire"

"Whatcha Need"

"Standing Water"

"Success Is Not So Sweet"

"The Great Exaggerator"

"Oxygen"

"Good for You"

"Slowly Rising"

"Fearless Leader"

Welcome to the Minority: The A+M Years, 1988–1991

(limited-edition compilation album)

RELEASED: AUGUST 2007

Label: Hip-O Select

Producers: Lenny Kaye, Soul Asylum, Steve Jordan

Hang Time complete album, plus bonus tracks "Just Plain Evil" and "It's Not My Fault"
    (written by Christopher Cerf and Sarah Durkee)

And the Horse They Rode in On complete album, plus bonus remix of "Something Out
    of Nothing"

Live concert recordings from Chicago and Ann Arbor, Michigan, October 1990

Delayed Reaction

RELEASED: JULY 17, 2012

Label: 429 Records

Producers: John Fields and Soul Asylum

"Gravity"

"Into the Light"

"The Streets"

"By the Way"

"Pipe Dream"

"Let's All Kill Each Other"

"Cruel Intentions"

"The Juice"

"Take Manhattan"

"I Should've Stayed in Bed"

Change of Fortune

RELEASED: MARCH 18, 2016

Label: Entertainment One

Producers: John Fields and Soul Asylum

"Supersonic"

"Can't Help It"

"Doomsday"

"Ladies Man"

"Moonshine"

"Make It Real"

"When I See You"

"Dealing"
"Don't Bother Me"
"Morgan's Dog"
"Change of Fortune"
"Cool"

Live from Liberty Lunch, Austin, TX, Thursday 12/3/92
(live album)
Recorded: December 3, 1992
RELEASED: APRIL 21, 2018
Label: Columbia/Legacy
Producers: Darren Salmieri and Thom Panunzio (original recordings)
"Without a Trace"
"All the King's Friends"
"Sometime to Return"
"Veil of Tears"
"Get on Out"
"Runaway Train"
"Black Gold"
"Cartoon" (written by Dan Murphy)
"Somebody to Shove"
"Nice Guys (Don't Get Paid)"
"April Fool"
"To Sir with Love" (written by Don Black and Mark London)
"Gullible's Travels" (written by Dan Murphy)
"Cry to Me" (written by Bert Berns)
"Keep It Up"
"99%"
"Closer to the Stars"

The Twin/Tone Years

(limited-edition compilation album)
RELEASED: NOVEMBER 23, 2018
Label: Omnivore Recordings
Producers: Peter Jesperson and Cheryl Pawelski
Say What You Will . . . Everything Can Happen complete album
Made to Be Broken complete album
While You Were Out complete album
Clam Dip and Other Delights complete EP, plus bonus tracks "Move Over" (written by Janis Joplin), "Juke Box Hero" (written by Lou Gramm and Mick Jones), "Saving Grace," "Forever and a Day" (demo from *Hang Time*), "There It Goes" (previously unreleased), and "Artificial Heart" (alternate demo version)
Twin/Town Extras, featuring Loud Fast Rules demos "Black and Blue," "Cocktails," and "Propaganda"; demos of "Bad Moon Rising" (written by John Fogerty) and "Happy," recorded as Proud Crass Fools; and "Long Way Home" (written by Dan Murphy), "Another World, Another Day" (alternate version), "Swingin'," "Can't Go Back" (written by Dan Murphy, alternate version), "Catch Me If You Can," "Song of the Terrorist," "To Go There," "Twenty Year Itch," "Lost In Your Face," and "Ramblin' Rose" (written by Marijohn Wilkin and Fred Burch)

Hurry Up and Wait

RELEASED: APRIL 18, 2020
Label: Blue Élan Records
Producers: John Fields and Soul Asylum
"The Beginning"
"If I Told You"
"Got It Pretty Good"
"Make Her Laugh"
"Busy Signals"
"Social Butterfly"
"Dead Letter"
"Landmines"
"Here We Go"
"Freezer Burn"
"Silent Treatment"
"Hopped Up Feelin'"
"Silly Things"